Mercedes-Benz Saloon Coupé

THE COMPLETE STORY

OTHER TITLES IN THE CROWOOD AUTOCLASSICS SERIES

Mercedes-Benz Saloon Coupé

THE COMPLETE STORY

NIK GREENE

THE CROWOOD PRESS

First published in 2021 by

The Crowood Press Ltd

Ramsbury, Marlborough

Wiltshire SN8 2HR

enquiries@crowood.com

www.crowood.com

British Library Cataloguing-in-Publication Data

A catalogue record for this book is available from the British Library.

ISBN 978 1 78500 933 4

Typeset by Jean Cussons Typesetting, Diss, Norfolk

Cover design by Sergey Tsvetkov

Printed and bound in India by Parksons Graphics Pvt. Ltd., Mumbai.

CONTENTS

ACKNOWLEDGEMENTS

As always, the archive department of Daimler Stuttgart has been a special resource of material – this year more than ever. The people involved with the archive have worked even harder (if it were possible to do so) to bring information to us by email and online due to the COVID-19 virus. I have missed my trip to the archives this year but hopefully will return soon.

Thank you to everyone at Crowood for turning my work into real books.

I also wish to thank Gerrit den Hollander for his treasured catalogue and brochure information; Harry Niemann for his valued assistance with research and amazing books; the Worshipful Company of Coachmakers and Coach Harness Makers for their assistance with carriage history and photographs; Stefan Dierkes for sharing his knowledge and information on the Pietro Frua estate and sharing his website http://www.pietro-frua.de; Paul and Sigrun Alice Bracq for their willingness to share; and Paolo Pininfarina for his time; my spaniel Troilus, who sits by my side in the spare chair every time I write; and last but never least, my dear wife Trudy for listening to my ramblings and watching the back of my head as I peer at my screens.

TIMELINE

CHAPTER ONE

EARLY AUTOMOTIVE HISTORY

The idea of self-propelled vehicles can be traced back as far as third-century China: during the construction of the Great Wall, workers used 'wheelbarrows' with sails to aid with transporting materials more quickly. Emperor Liang Yuan Ti (fifth century AD) also documented that he built a wind chariot capable of transporting thirty men over several hundred *li* in one day (1 *li* = 500m or 600yd).

Leonardo da Vinci, some time around the year 1478, drew plans for his own self-propelled cart, which was powered by coiled springs and also featured steering and brake capabilities. It is uncertain whether it was actually built, but it was said to be a special attraction at the Renaissance festivals. The regulator mechanism, like that of a more modern differential, propelled the vehicle forward smoothly at the release of a lever, while the steering was programmable to go either straight or at pre-set angles. In 2006, Italy's Institute and Museum of the History of Science in Florence built a working model based on da Vinci's design and, to the surprise of many, the cart worked.

One of the most famous examples of a self-propelled vehicle – thanks to an engraving rich in valuable information – is that of the mathematician Simon Thévenin, who was born in Bruges in 1548. He built a sailing cart for the 'grandees of the court of the Prince of Orange to enjoy themselves'.

The chronicler of the time Jean de la Varende reported that twenty-eight people climbed into this sailing cart, amongst whom were the ambassadors of the emperor, the great lords of France, England, Denmark and even an illustrious prisoner, Admiral Don Francisco of Mendoza. The 'flying chariot' managed to travel an estimated distance of 75km (47 miles) in less than two hours at an average speed of around 37km/h (23mph); it actually reached 60km/h (37mph) and

TOP: **Workers on the Great Wall of China used wind and sail to assist with barrow propulsion.** BOTTOM: **Gaocang Wu Shu succeeded in building a wind chariot. There was another built in about AD 610 for the Emperor Yang of Sui (r. 604–617), as described in the *Continuation of the New Discourses on the Talk of the Times*.**

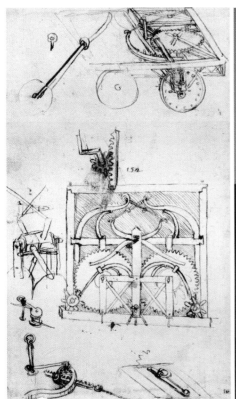

Leonard da Vinci's own 'self-propelled' cart (left) with the 2006 working model built by the Institute and Museum of the History of Science in Florence.

at one point the speed ignited the axles. The Thévenin chariot was exhibited at the Museum of Newport.

In 1769, Nicholas-Joseph Cugnot invented the first powered vehicle in history capable of transporting passengers, named the Cugnot in honour to its creator. It was a heavy three-wheeled vehicle purposely built from timber, and it was powered by a 2-cylinder steam engine that needed a huge boiler attached to the front. The single front wheel worked like a guide wheel to steer the vehicle on its course. All this made the vehicle extremely slow and difficult to drive, but nevertheless it appeared thirty years before the invention of the first steam locomotive.

Cugnot started a trend, and for the next forty years or so there were a

The Thévenin chariot.

Nicholas-Joseph Cugnot's steam powered vehicle appeared thirty years before the invention of the first steam locomotive.

number of 'steam-powered' carriages, including that of Richard Trevithick in 1801, which became known fondly as the 'Puffing Devil Road Locomotive'. Although it became a precursor to the railway steam engine, the engineering principles of external combustion contributed greatly to the development of the hydrogen-powered internal combustion engine of François Isaac de Rivaz in 1807.

The horseless carriage went through many variations in power source, including compressed air, hydrogen, oil and even electric motors, but it wasn't until German inventor

and engineer Siegfried Marcus that a motorized carriage powered by an internal combustion engine became a reality.

The idea for Marcus's first car, in around 1864–5, apparently came to him by chance while he was considering the production of illumination by igniting a mixture of gasoline and air with a stream of sparks. The reaction was so violent that it occurred to him to use it as a power source.

His first vehicle was a handcart that married a two-cycle, one-cylinder engine geared to the rear wheels without any intervening clutch. To start it, it was necessary to have a strong man lift the rear end while the wheels were spun, after which it ran for about 180m (600ft). Marcus was so dissatisfied at its performance, however, that he dismantled it and didn't return to it until ten years later due to a multitude of other commitments. These included patenting in the mid-1870s his 'rotating brush carburettor' device that would convert raw fuel to gas and mix with air to create a clean internal combustion, and adding to this in 1883 a patent for a low-voltage ignition magneto, enabling an efficient new petrol engine to be built.

In 1888–9, Märky, Bromovsky & Schulz built another car from scratch for Marcus, making him instantly famous throughout the world. The heavy vehicle, made of wood and iron, was not particularly suited to the uneven tracks and roads, but with the recently patented magneto-electric ignition and the spray brush carburettor used on the four-stroke engine, it made the engine extremely convenient and reliable for the day. It had a capacity of 1570cu cm, an output of approx. 0.75hp and generated a speed of around 6–8km/h (4–5mph).

Thirty-five years after Marcus died, and soon after Hitler came to power, the Nazi regime attempted to destroy any evidence of Jewish success, so all record of the inventor's achievements, blueprints, files and patents were destroyed, including a monument honouring Marcus at the Vienna Technical University. In 1950, however, Marcus's second car was found where it had been hidden: bricked up behind a false wall of a Viennese museum by employees to protect it from Nazi destruction. So robust was this car that

Cylinder

Equipage
des pompes

Hydogen Fuel Balloon

Piston

Ignition Spark

Piston

Opposing Piston
valve for
air in and gases out

Hydrogen Fuel
Balloon

Handle for
Valve Piston

Handle for Valve Piston

The hydrogen-powered internal combustion engine of François Isaac de Rivaz in 1807.

LEFT: **Siegfried Marcus's 1864 motorized carriage, powered by an internal combustion engine.** RIGHT: **The Märky, Bromovsky & Schulz horseless carriage built in 1888.**

when it was retrieved it was still possible to drive it. In fact, it remains operable to this day and is now owned by the Austrian Automobile, Motorcycle and Touring Club in Vienna and on display at the Vienna Technical Museum; once in a while, it has even been seen trundling the streets of the city.

Most early vehicles, not to mention those that only existed on paper, were small, self-propelled carriages that were not capable of transporting people. As much as Siegfried Marcus achieved, when questioned he expressed the opinion that his vehicles would never succeed commercially and essentially further development was 'a senseless waste of time and effort'.

Although Marcus can be credited with perhaps building the first purpose-constructed automobile with a 'petrol internal combustion engine' it has been accepted that his invention was purely an intellectual curiosity, and, just as he made clear, he had no interest in developing the 'motor car' to be become anything more.

If the horseless carriage were to become anything more than just an experiment, it needed more devotion and tenacity to develop it further. Karl Benz may not have been the first inventor of the motor car, but his greatest achievement lay in the tenacity with which he developed his idea of a 'horseless carriage' into a product for everyday use, which he then brought to market and made accessible for the entire world – unlike any of the other inventors mentioned here.

CHAPTER TWO

THE AGE OF THE MOTOR CAR

To change the way people thought about travel required so much more than just an engine driving wheels, whether it was a cart or purpose-made frame. People already had a perfectly decent way of getting around with their carriages and horses, and all they had to do was to feed and care for their horses, so why change the power source from a reliable horse to some new-fangled and potentially unreliable motor? Initially it was thought that the cheaper and simpler source of power that the Lenoir two-stroke engine could provide would only be of benefit to 'others', like boat and static farm implement manufacturers, and it would never be used as a mode of transport, yet it was

The Étienne Lenoir two-stroke engine.

The Hippomobile was powered by a substance dubbed 'town gas', a mixture consisting of around 50 per cent hydrogen, plus carbon dioxide, nitrogen and methane. Approximately 600 such machines were sold.

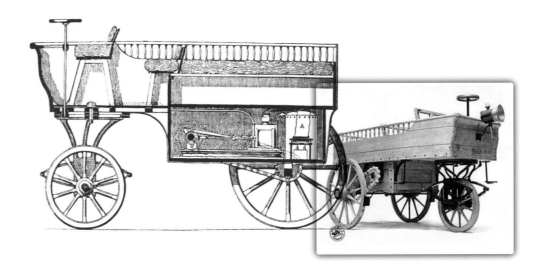

essentially this that eventually drove the advancement and development of the internal combustion engine.

Lenoir's attempt at a 'gas-powered vehicle', known inauspiciously as the Hippomobile, was merely a carriage placed on top of tricycle frame. However, it was a wake-up call to the public and played an important part in exciting the engineers to improve things.

It was Nicolaus Otto's four-stroke engine that contributed to what would be a huge leap forward for the potential automotive world. Although initially, due to its cumbersome size and slow stroke speed, it was considered only as a stationary power source, by 1885 two of his engineers, Gottlieb Daimler and Wilhelm Maybach, had managed to develop a more compact 1.5hp vertical 'high-speed' engine with a 600rpm capability that turned things over.

The age of the 'motor car' was started primarily by the contributions made by Karl Benz and Emile Levassor, not because of their engines or even the contraption to which they were attached, but because for the first time they made the concept of the automobile commercially feasible.

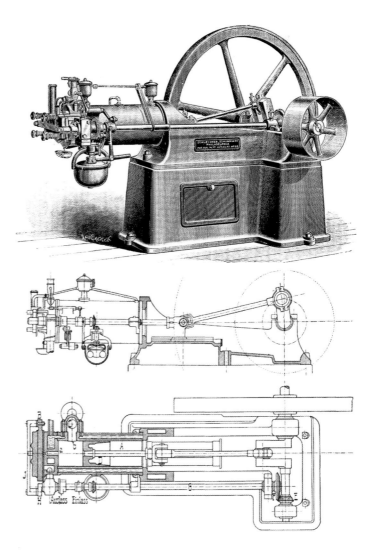

The Nicolaus Otto four-stroke stationary engine of 1876.

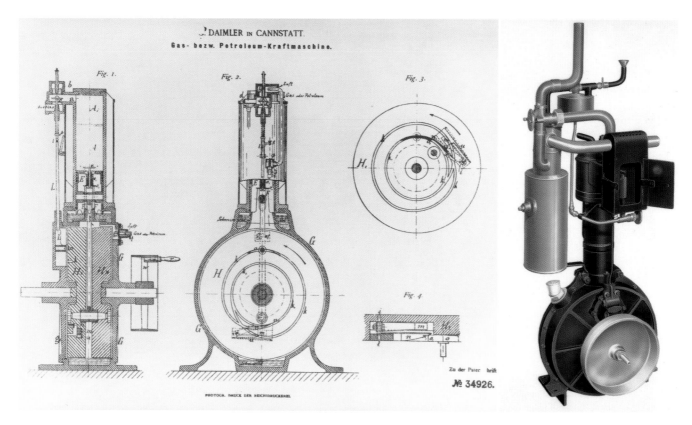

Daimler and Maybach succeeded in developing and building a considerably more compact and upright version of the Otto four-stroke engine; it was later referred to as the 'Grandfather Clock' due to its shape.

The reason perhaps that Benz succeeded, albeit sixty years after the first tentative steps into building 'motor cars', where all those others fell by the wayside was down to timing. Just before Benz made his auto, the modern bicycle had come into being, and this brought the possibility of individual, independent transportation into the public's imagination.

THE SALOON COUPÉ BEGINNING

At the time there were carriages with a multitude of names for a multitude of purposes, from small shooting carriages to full long-distance travelling coaches. However, as with many things in history, defining moments are made by changes in necessity as much as fashion.

The 'Berlin' (later the 'Berline') was a case in point. The carriage was designed around 1660 or 1670 by a Piedmon-

tese architect commissioned by the general quartermaster to Frederick William, Elector of Brandenburg. The Elector would often travel from Berlin to the French capital of Paris and needed an enclosed comfortable carriage to do the long journey.

On its very first trip to Paris, his carriage created a sensation. While heavy-duty vehicles had used double-railed frames before, passenger vehicles normally only had a single rail. Its strength and ride made it more convenient than other carriages of the time and, being lighter and more controllable, it was far less likely to overturn.

The elegant but durable style was soon widely copied and was officially named 'Berlin style' after the city from which the carriage had come (French 'Berline'). It quickly replaced the less practical and less comfortable state coaches and gala coaches in the seventeenth century and was consequently adapted and altered in many ways, often with a view to enhancing elegance of shape, with superior compactness and convenience.

KARL FRIEDRICH BENZ

Born: 25 November 1844, Mühlburg, Germany
Died: 4 April 1929, Ladenburg, Germany

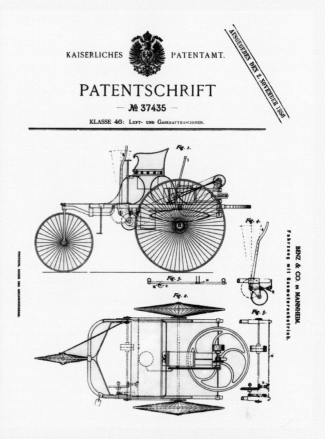

Karl Benz alongside what has become known as the 'birth certificate' of the automobile.

Karl Benz built his first motor car with a single-cylinder, four-stroke engine, and a patent was granted on 29 January 1886. This patent, No. 37435, granted by the imperial patent office for his 'vehicle with gas-engine drive' was to be the automobile's birth certificate.

Karl Benz did not content himself with simply outfitting an existing carriage with an engine: his engine, drivetrain and chassis were designed from the ground up. His design and layout of engine, ignition, cooling, transmission, wheels and brakes became the standard for every automobile built since then.

So fierce was the competition at the time to produce a motor car that Benz worked tirelessly in fear that another inventor would beat him to it.

During testing and before the patent had been granted, he only dared to go out on the road at night and only around the immediate neighbourhood of his factory, which, being in an industrial area, was luckily deserted. Night after night, he progressively learned to take command of his vehicle and its technology, cautiously extending the length of the drives he took with it, until on Sunday, 3 July 1886, he took a drive around the ramparts surrounding Mannheim.

He rattled around the town at a steady 15km/h (9mph) with his son Eugen running alongside the vehicle with a bottle of

This will always be remembered as the first practical motor car.

A comparison of the Benz patent motor car from 1888 (left) and the world's first automobile from 1886.

gasoline to keep it fuelled; baffled onlookers stood aghast at the strange tricycle, and the next day all Mannheim talked about Karl Benz and his invention. The single-minded determination Karl Benz showed when he developed his idea of a 'horseless vehicle' into a product suitable for daily use, and made his vision a reality, was his crucial achievement. He had the idea of a motor car, designed it, built it, tested it, patented it, marketed it, produced it in series, developed it further, and thus made his innovation usable.

His third model, a slightly revised version to make it more marketable, was exhibited in 1887 at the Paris Exposition and almost immediately sold to a Frenchman by the name of Emile Roger, a fortuitous meeting that resulted in him becoming an agent based in Paris. For the first time motor cars were being offered for sale to the public.

For Type III, there was a return to the wooden wheel as the public were unsure of the more fragile wire wheel. Different body types were also available. For instance, the customer could choose an additional vis-à-vis bench and thus have four seats all together, or he could choose a folding cover.

For the record, it was this model that Bertha Benz used to go on her 'long-distance trip' from Mannheim to Pforzheim (88km/55 miles).

Karl Benz had not wasted any time on the design of a steering system but had gone for a simple three-wheeler to start with, while Daimler had opted for the age-old carriage 'fifth wheel' system. Neither Benz nor Daimler knew that, as early as 1816, carriage builder Georg Lankensperger in Munich had been granted a 'privilege', as patents were called at the time, for a 'steering device for horse-drawn vehicles'. It was only by coincidence that Karl Benz came across this privilege when browsing through a trade journal in 1891, specifying that 'the extended lines of the wheel axes must converge in the centre point of the bend'. He realized the significance of this design for the automobile, and double-pivot steering was to become the solution to the automotive steering problem. His own 'axle-pivot steering' solution paved the way for a safe and reliable steering system and from then on he moved to four-wheeled vehicles, his first being the Victoria, which was also available as a four-seated version with face-to-face seat benches, the Vis-à-Vis.

A close look at Type III showed significant differences marking technological progress over the preceding models and simultaneously making it more suitable for serial production. The vehicle had two forward speeds, the wheel spokes were made of wood instead of wire, the wooden body was completely separated from the chassis, the engine was encapsulated, and the steering was improved, along with a sprung front wheel.

The Benz 'axle-pivot steering' patent (DRP 73151) was granted on 28 February 1893.

Both variations were equipped with a horizontally installed one-cylinder engine with vertical flywheel; displacement and performance were continuously enlarged up to the end of production in 1900.

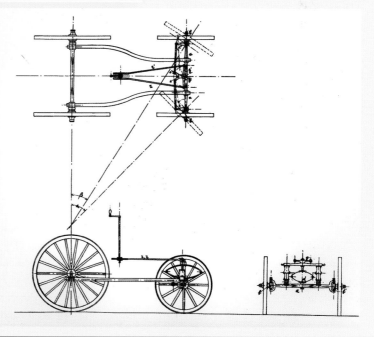

GOTTLIEB WILHELM DAIMLER

Born: 17 March 1834, Schorndorf, Germany
Died: 6 March 1900, Stuttgart, Germany

Daimler and Maybach had been developing the internal combustion engine, initially for Nicholas Otto, but later under their own direction in his conservatory workshop in Cannstatt.

On 16 December 1883, they patented the first of their engines, fuelled by ligroin, a volatile solvent extracted from petroleum. It achieved Daimler's goal of being small and running fast enough to be useful at 750rpm. Improvements over the next four years brought that up to 900rpm. Daimler had three engines built to this design early in 1884, and a flywheel was included in one of the engines. This design was smaller and lighter than engines by other inventors of the time and was called the 'Grandfather Clock', having achieved the goals of producing a throttling engine with high enough rpm while being small enough to be used in transportation. Daimler and Maybach built the 1884 engine into a two-wheeled test frame, which was patented as the 'Petroleum Reitwagen' (petroleum riding car).

Independently of one another, Karl Benz and Gottlieb Daimler each produced an automobile in 1886, both in Germany, about 100km (60 miles) apart.

On 8 March 1886, Gottlieb Daimler secretly ordered a carriage in the version 'Americaine' from the coachbuilder Wilhelm Wimpff & Sohn, ostensibly as a present for his wife Emma's forthcoming birthday, but in fact to install an engine into it. A 1.1hp air-cooled version of the previous one-cylinder 'Grandfather Clock' was installed by a German engineering company called Maschinenfabrik Esslingen. The engine power was transmitted by a set of belts and, during testing on the roads to Untertürkheim, it became the first four-wheeled vehicle to reach 16km/h (10mph).

In 1887, the cooling method for the motor carriage was changed from air to water, with a large-surfaced finned radiator mounted underneath the rear seats.

Although Daimler's motor vehicle was the first four-wheel vehicle driven by a high-speed combustion engine, it was merely considered a carriage without shaft or horses. Daimler had not given any thought to an evolution model or even the series production of his motor vehicle – he merely wanted to demonstrate the possible ways of using his engine and carried on looking for alternatives.

In 1886, his engine was mounted to a longboat and achieved a speed of 6 knots (11km/h or 7mph). This was the first motorboat, and boat engines became Daimler's main product for several years. To allay the first customers' fears that the

The petroleum riding car was simply a test-bed to demonstrate the feasibility of a liquid petroleum engine using a compressed fuel charge to power a vehicle.

The Daimler 'motor coach', built in 1886, seen here with both Gottlieb and his son Adolf Daimler.

The petrol engine rapidly became the power of choice for boat engines.

On 10 August 1888, Leipzig-based bookseller Dr Karl Wölfert took off in a motorized airship from the factory yard of the Daimler Motor Company at the Seelberg in Cannstatt for a flight to Kornwestheim. The drive system was the famous single-cylinder Daimler engine with an output of 2hp (1.5kW), which powered two propellers: one in a vertical position and the other horizontal.

The single-cylinder engine went on to be used in streetcars and trolleybuses.

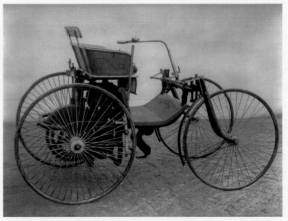

The Stahlradwagen (wire-wheeled car).

petroleum fuelled engine could explode, Daimler hid the engine under a ceramic cover and told them it was 'oil-electrical'.

With a growing reputation for safety and reliability, the engine was primarily used in 'commercial vehicles'.

In 1889, Daimler and Maybach built the 'Stahlradwagen' (wire-wheeled car), their first automobile that did not involve adapting a horse-drawn carriage with their engine, but which was somewhat influenced by bicycle designs. There was no production in Germany, but it was licensed to be built in France and presented to the public in Paris in October 1889 by both engineers.

Daimler Motoren Gesellschaft (DMG) was founded on 28 November 1890, with Maybach as chief designer. Its purpose was the construction of small, high-speed engines for use in land, water and air transport. The three uses were expressed by Daimler in a sketch that became the basis for a logo with a three-pointed star. No one at the DMG corporation had any faith in a profitable market for the automobile, however, and after many company 'stockholder' disagreements and battles, DMG didn't manage to sell a single automobile until 1892. They resigned their shares and places at DMG, although eventually the pair were reinstated into the corporation, primarily to aid with producing a new automobile based on their new Phoenix 2-cylinder engine.

Daimler and Maybach continued to work together and develop engines and engine technology using the abandoned conservatory at the Hermann Hotel as their workshop.

Over its lifespan it was cut longitudinally and latitudinally; it was halved and quartered; the front was cut off, the top cut off – in fact, it was cut about in every manner that fancy could devise. When the Berlin was cut in halves longitudinally, the resulting vehicle was called the 'Vis-à-Vis', a term later adopted by both Daimler and Benz, in which form it accommodated two persons sitting face to face.

When the process of cutting was carried still further, and the Vis-à-Vis was also cut down latitudinally, the Berlin was so dismembered that only one quarter of it remained; this vehicle was, appropriately, called a 'Desobligeant', or 'Disobliger', as it could take one passenger only and if anyone asked for a ride they were disobliged. The slightly bigger version with two seats, the 'Carrosse-Coupé' or 'Berlingot', when first used for travel was nicknamed 'Diligence', on account of the speed with which it performed the journey from Paris to Calais.

Although the term 'coupé' was never really used in England, the English did borrow the style from the French coupé, which was generally referred to as the 'dress chariot'. It was based on this carriage that Lord Chancellor Henry Brougham, a fashion-forward gentleman, designed his very own four-wheeled, one-horse carriage that became extremely popular during the 1800s.

The brougham appeared as if the front were cut away, preserving only the two doors of the rear section of a coach body. Designed to be cosy and intimate, it had one forward-facing seat for two passengers with sometimes one, sometimes two, fold-away coachman's seats at the front corners where extra passengers could also ride, and it usually had a glazed front window through which passengers could see forward.

There were many variations on this design, such as the

The original plain and simple Berlin carriage.

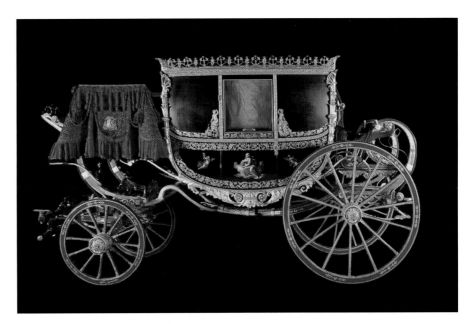

The Berlin of the Cardinale Luciano Luigi Bonaparte shows how elaborate style became over time.

country brougham and depot brougham. Due to their neat size and compactness, many broughams were later converted into hacks (town taxis) called 'growlers'. One style of coupé carriage even had a folding child's seat inside, facing backwards. Another was slightly longer, with a full-framed seat inside the front of the body, and was called a clarence.

The top carriage was referred to as the 'Disobliger' due to there only being enough room for one passenger. As a wider version it was the first carriage to use the term 'Carrosse-Coupé' (cut body).

BELOW: **The original 'British' version of the coupé body was always referred to as the brougham.**

The brougham style went on to be used in automobile categories. This Rolls-Royce was known as the brougham landaulet.

In the USA, both the coupé and the clarence were also known as extension-front broughams.

The innovative design proved very popular and became an instant success with middle-class and wealthy families. Unlike the high, heavy, bulky coaches of the time, the brougham was a light and compact carriage, cheaper to buy and ideal for travelling around busy streets; it also claims the distinction of being the first to have elliptical springs.

Many carriage manufacturing companies built brougham styles in varying sizes that would accommodate from two to four passengers. It went on to influence the construction of carriages across the whole world and even early car designs – the brougham name also went on to be used by several automobile manufacturers such as Rolls-Royce, Studebaker, General Motors, Cadillac and Ford.

The landau carriage was a four-wheeled carriage invented in Germany that seated four people on two facing seats (vis à vis) with an elevated front seat for the coachman. It was distinguished by two folding hoods, one at each end, which met at the top to form a box-like enclosure with side windows. It was a heavy vehicle, often drawn by a team of four horses, and was widely used from the eighteenth century in England. Usually these landau carriages were severely cut away underneath at each end, so that the bottom of the door was the lowest point of the carriage body for ease of access.

From the landau came the landaulet, or landaulette; appearing as if the front were cut away, with a forward-facing seat for two people, this was often referred to as the 'landau coupé', which really could be the origin of the coupé convertible automobile.

The landau carriage had two tonneaus for closed or open-air travel whereas the landaulet only had one at the rear.

23

CHAPTER THREE

THE COUPÉ AUTOMOBILE

Once the motor car took hold in the minds of the general public, its move away from carriage and bicycle design was swift; however, as is often the case with technical consumables, the shape remained more about form through development and function. The shape of a motor car's frontal area in the early days of development is a case in point. Engines were in the rear, so all it needed up front was space for driver and passenger and a means to steer. Once the more

efficient water-cooled engines took over from earlier air-cooled ones, it was found that for a more efficient cooling effect the radiator needed to be in the front, which then needed protecting from the elements.

Then it was decided to fit the engine in the front, which extended the area at the front further; then, in addition to the actual shape constraints, other aspects came to include the choice of materials, touch and feel, and the greatest ease of use. All of these factors became more than just function, and the outward appearance started to reflect the inner values of the product, such as reliability, innovation and emotion. The design of an automobile became exciting and eye-catching and, as well as reflecting the value of the brand, it started to reflect the values of its owner.

Another factor in the early design paradigm was that after the initial excitement of owning and driving a 'motor car' had subsided, many of the designs were geared towards being chauffeur driven. Eventually, open-top motoring gave way to some kind of roof lining, very often nothing much more than a simple frame covered in canvas to protect the passengers from

The Daimler 3 HP taxi was step two in the advancement of cooling the engine. The copper tank of water with a zigzag of pipes can be clearly seen under the front.

Even though the Panhard & Levassor still followed the Carrosse-Coupé in style, the third step into advancing the engine cooling can clearly be seen here, reshaping the front.

the elements; but then, in the same way as the conventional horse-drawn carriage became a Berlin-style, closed-form carriage, so too did the automobile. This ensured a degree of privacy, comfort and security for its passengers while the chauffeur sat atop to drive the automobile.

Large, cumbersome, chauffeur-driven vehicles were all well and good when travelling for business or from town to town, but for local trips, something else was needed; just in the same way as the horse-drawn Berlin needed the neater coupé, the large motor vehicle needed a similarly truncated version too.

What became the coupé design owes much of its body form to that of the horse-drawn landaulet or, as it was sometimes known, the half-landau. The coachman sat on a

box seat far in front of the passenger compartment and was generally out in the open, only later protected by means of a windscreen. Behind the chauffeur was often (but not always) a hard covering over an elegant compartment with a glass top or a front windshield. The rear section, as in the landau, was often a drop-down hood. The landaulet was always a custom-built carriage, which made it very exclusive.

At the end of the nineteenth century, the customary distinction in coach construction between the landau and landaulet was naturally carried over into automotive design, both Daimler and Benz initially making cars with landaulet and landau bodies. The Daimler Victoria was offered with a landaulet body, and one such vehicle became the world's very first taxi when a Stuttgart-based haulage and taxi-

The Daimler Victoria was offered with a landaulet body, and one such vehicle became the world's very first taxi.

cab operator, Friedrich August Greiner, ordered a Victoria landaulet with a taximeter from Daimler-Motoren-Gesellschaft (DMG) under order No. 1329. The vehicle was duly delivered in May 1897, and the world's first motorized taxi went into service in June, once the required permit had been obtained from the police. The vehicle cost its owner the small fortune of 5,530 marks. Included in that price were the landaulet half-convertible top, two dash leather coverings, reverse gear and solid rubber tyres.

In the following decades, both Daimler and Benz supplied taxis based on this distinctive body design. However, it was likely that this vehicle design contributed to the later unpopularity of the landaulet with the public. No well-to-do VIP wanted to look as though they were driving or being driven in a taxi, not to mention that etiquette at the time was that driving on business or in town should be done in an enclosed limousine. If you owned a landaulet, it should be used outside the city or town for pleasure drives.

Its evolving body shape, physically and technically as well as in genre, can be considered as a direct relative to the coupé's closed, cosseted body style, with its hand-crafted elegant, cut-down version of a limousine. Each design focused exclusively on the passengers; more often than not, these vehicles didn't even have space for luggage – if needed, this would have been transported in a separate baggage cart. The role of each coupé model was to offer an intimate atmosphere and exude style, elegance and luxury in every way. Being chauffeur driven was not enough – eventually the sophisticated coupés evolved, while maintaining their reputation for luxury, to being driven by one of the passengers themselves.

Mercedes-Benz coupés became the embodiment of elegance and exclusivity on four wheels. Their design became an experience for all the senses, appealing to every emotion. Hans-Dieter Futschik, the designer responsible for many of the later Mercedes-Benz models, said:

A shorter wheelbase compared with the saloons gives it different proportions that are almost sports car-like in character. The passenger compartment is set further back. This gives it a sportier look than a saloon. In addition, the greenhouse is smaller and more streamlined than the basic body. It looks like a small head set on a muscular body, exuding a powerful and more dynamic attitude. The arched roof line and closed side panels without B-pillars and window frames create exciting and elegantly fluid lines. Everything radiates power, elegance and agility.

THE LANDAULET

The body form of the landaulet, or half-landau, owes much to the construction of horse-drawn coaches. The landau (or sometimes 'Landauer' in German) was an open coach, prob-

The 20/35 HP Benz landaulet from 1909.

The 8/20 HP Benz of 1912.

ably named after the town of Landau in the Palatinate region of Germany. The passengers sat facing each other, and could be protected by two half-roof sections, pulled over them from either end of the vehicle when required. The coachman sat on a box seat, well away from the passenger compartment. The landaulet structure differed in that it only had the rear half-roof covering. Depending on the design, the driver's compartment in front of the passenger seats could have a rigid roof, a glass top or a front windshield.

At the end of the nineteenth century, the customary distinction in coach construction between the landau and landaulet was carried over into automotive design, with Daimler and Benz both initially making cars with landaulet and landau bodies. It was also the foundation of what would later become the coupé automobile body.

During the first half of the twentieth century, even though there was still no consistent or standard design model, the landaulet design emerged as the accepted form, and became increasingly popular with customers. One of the reasons

for this was that as speeds increased, passengers became more reluctant to sit with their backs to the direction of travel and also wanted a greater degree of protection from the elements.

One of the major points of difference was in the area of the driver's seat. The box seat of the Daimler belt-driven taxi landaulet of 1896 left the driver completely unprotected. In comparison, a 20/35 HP Benz landaulet from 1909 offered the driver a windshield and a rigid roof, albeit without doors or side windows. Side doors were added in the 8/20 HP Benz of 1912, but still no windows.

Subsequent landaulet models reversed the principle of leaving the chauffeur out in the open, protecting the driver with a windshield on all sides, as in a limousine, while the folding convertible top over the rear seats continued to offer flexibility for the passengers.

The folding convertible top design as a luxury variation on the automobile was discussed by authors Ernst Misol and Hermann Klaiber in 1913 in their book entitled 'What

This more contemporary form of the landaulet was used in luxury models such as the
15/70/100 HP Mercedes-Benz 400 Pullman landaulet from the late 1920s.

On taking delivery of his V140 in person in 1997, Pope John Paul II was given a
briefing on the car's technical features and praised the design.

The W100 600 landaulet was used by many heads of state.

do I need to know about my car, and how should I drive it to comply with the authorities' regulations?' Misol and Klaiber emphasized the advantages of different body styles for different purposes: 'A luxury car used only in city traffic should always have a fully enclosed body, that is the limousine design. But for shorter journeys outside city limits, preference is to be given to the landaulet with its retractable top at the rear.'

Owners of luxury landaulet cars in the pre-World War I period included Emperor Wilhelm II. The emperor's first vehicle of this type was a 39/75 HP Mercedes chain-driven landaulet, which he used as a travelling car. This was followed in 1911 by a 38/70 HP Mercedes landaulet for the

same purpose. The Emperor then chose a 28/60 HP Mercedes landaulet as a city car in 1913. And during a visit by the heir to the Romanian throne in 1913, the monarch and his guest were driven through the streets in a 26/65 HP Mercedes-Knight landaulet.

Following the end of the imperial era, in 1938 Mercedes-Benz presented Paul von Hindenburg with a 12/55 HP Mercedes-Benz 300 six-seater landaulet; Hindenburg had been elected as president of the Weimar Republic in 1925, as the successor to Friedrich Ebert.

The landaulet went on to become the quintessence of VIP motoring, used by monarchs dignitaries and celebrities all over the world.

The landaulet taxicabs based on the Mercedes-Benz 260 D from 1936. Although at first the body style was connected with the common taxi, its design soon became associated with the elite.

CHAPTER FOUR

PRE-MERGER BENZ

Things changed very quickly for Karl Benz in the first two years of the existence of his 'Patent Motorwagen'. Having essentially built the vehicle from scratch with no intention of marketing it, when it came to adapting it commercially, any changes he made were almost a redesign – unlike the Daimler 'Carriage', where the basic structure already existed.

Marketing his contraption meant offering refinements. Wheels were changed from the original wire spoke and constructed in wood, essentially to cope better with the rough conditions of the tracks and roadways. The front wheel was given a spring on which to support the front of the carriage floor to offer a bit more comfort. A leather mudflap was offered as well as a tonneau hood to protect

The Benz Victoria Vis-à-Vis.

The Benz Victoria Vis-à-Vis, offering sun cover. Hanging on to horse-drawn carriage names and designs, it was offered with a phaeton and landau body.

from rain and dirt. The Mk 3 version also had its engine enclosed with bodywork that formed around the seat in what was essentially the first purpose-made body design. The first firewall appeared at the front when no rear facing seat was needed, and better brakes were added.

The original prototype engine size of 0.75hp was increased to 1.5, 2.5 and eventually 3hp. Between 1886 and 1894, Benz managed to sell twenty-five units of all the engines.

With the design of an effective axle-pivot (king-pin) steering system (patent No. DRP 73151, from 28 February 1893), the way was paved for four-wheeled vehicles, and from 1893, Benz introduced a four-seat option that was to be called the Benz Victoria or Vis-à-Vis (face to face).

THE INFLUENCE OF THE BICYCLE

Neither the original Patent Wagen nor the Victoria were commercial successes, and this was largely put down to the fact that, as advanced as they were in engineering terms,

appearance wise they still resembled carriages and ultimately many carriage owners saw little reason to change from horse power to engine power just for the sake of it.

A close friend of Karl Benz and business owner himself, by the name of Josef Brecht, encouraged Benz to return to his bicycle beginnings. Just before the Benz Patentwagen was introduced, there was a boom in the 'safety bicycle': it had become almost de rigueur and chic to be seen riding one through towns and cities. During the early 1890s, Europe had suffered from a quite severe economic turndown so bicycles were popular with the not so wealthy. The well-off adopted them too, however, and according to Brecht, there were those who would adorn their cycles with jewels and have them covered in gold leaf. It would be these that a cycle-influenced motor car would appeal to.

Brecht got his way and the Benz 'Velocipede' was the result. It was an instant hit. Far smaller and lighter than the previous Victoria, it was also half the price.

One of the reasons it deserves a mention in this coupé book is through the development of design.

By the end of the 1890s, Benz was being put under pres-

Later renamed the 'Stahlradwagen', or wire-wheeled car (right), 500 were sold in
the first two years, with a total of 1,200 built between 1894 and 1901.

sure by other manufacturers, including Daimler, to move
away from both velo and carriage design idioms, and in 1898
a new range of models was introduced to attempt at leaving
the horse-drawn carriage image behind. The Benz 'Dos-à-
Dos' was named due to its more convenient seating arrangement of two rows of bench seats either back to back or both
facing forward.

All of these models were equipped with the new Benz
engine called the 'Contra-Motor'; due to its boxer-style
flat cylinder configuration with its 'governor flywheel' in a
vertical position, it marked a change in both refinement
and power, producing between 5 and 20hp. These more
powerful engines needed bigger and more efficient radia-
tors, and this meant moving the radiator to the front of the

vehicle and designing a cowl over the top to concentrate
the rate of air flow – changing the shape of the automobile
for ever.

THE CONTRA-MOTOR

Time and time again, August Horch, who lived through the
years of motor vehicle development at Benz, tried to con-
vince 'Papa Benz', as he always called him, of the necessity
of performance increases. On one occasion he was even
successful, when he was given a free hand on the original
single-cylinder engine and managed to squeeze an extra 1hp
by changing the compression.

The Dos-à-Dos arrangement marked a change to a more conventional seating pattern.

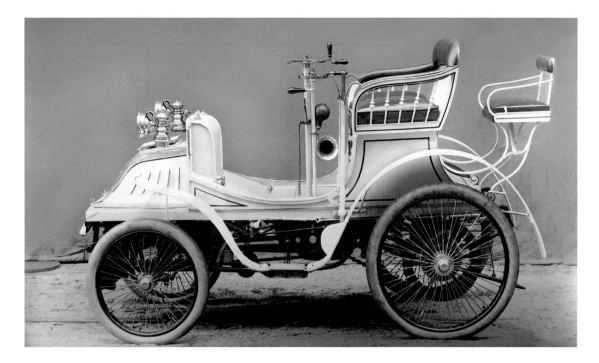

The Dos-à-Dos Elegant, with its front-position radiator, defined the shape of all future automobiles.

EMILE ROGER

Born: 17 December 1850, Châteauvillain, France
Died: 25 November 1898, Châteauvillain, France
Emile Louis Roger was born in the town of Châteauvillain in northeast France in 1850, the son of Edme-Marcel Roger, a farmer from Latrecey, and Alexandrine Aubriot.

A rare image of Emile Roger. In July 1894, Roger participated in the first international competition of horse-free vehicles, on the road from Paris to Rouen, where he obtained fifth prize.

To the disappointment of his father, he chose not to work the land of his family but to pursue as a designer in Paris. He entered the School of Arts and Crafts of Châlons-sur-Marne in 1866 and worked, first as a designer in the workshops of the Fives Cail company in Lille, specializing in works and railway equipment, and later at Letestu as a pump designer.

At the age of twenty he was called upon to fight in the Franco-Prussian war against Germany. Achieving the rank of sergeant-major on 1 January 1871, he was released from his military obligations on 26 October of the same year after the war's end.

By 1879, he was the director of the Locomotive Rental Company and in 1883 established himself at 52 rue des Dames in Paris, manufacturing gas and oil engines.

In late 1887, the world changed with one simple purchase, a Benz Patentwagen.

The French engineer saw one of the first three-wheelers at the Benz workshops in Mannheim and immediately recognized the potential of this invention as well as its marketability. Karl Benz said, 'After a trial run and having had the operation and control of the car explained by me, Monsieur Roger saw to the shipment of the car, paid for it and took off with his purchase.' By the spring of 1888, the Frenchman was granted the sole agency rights for the sale of all Benz vehicles and engines in France. Roger was not only a high-performing sales partner for Karl Benz, selling vehicles from Germany with great success; this step also marked the beginning of foreign sales worldwide for Benz.

In these early years, Karl Benz had trouble finding buyers of his vehicles domestically, and it was only the success of his invention in the French market that allowed him to start series production.

By 1893, Benz had sold some 60 per cent of the total of sixty-nine cars produced to French customers; by the turn of the

Sales promotion in the early days: a newspaper ad placed by Emile Roger in 1888. On the left, a Benz patent motor car is depicted, which was marketed highly successfully by Roger.

century, he had supplied about a third of the total production volume of over 2,300 automobiles to Emile Roger. Roger's marketing strategy was successful. He used the numerous racing events in those days to publicize the fact 'his' cars, unlike competitors', made it to the finishing line and occupied top places. However, he conveniently 'forgot' to mention the name Benz and in 1896, out of spite, Karl Benz sent his own to participate in the long-distance Paris–Marseille–Paris rally. Two cars, a Vis-à-Vis and a phaeton, were built under his personal supervision. Of the fifty cars lined up at the start, just nine crossed the finishing line, with the two Benz cars finishing ahead of the Roger Benz.

Now that Benz had provided proof of his cars' reliability, 200 orders for the Velocipede were received in a matter of days. According to the order books for the Benz patent motor car, kept in the archives of Daimler AG, Benz supplied 121 cars to France in 1897 – twice as many as in the preceding year.

One example of Roger's 'patent motor car' No. 3 of 1888, which was undoubtedly presented at the 1889 World Exposition in Paris, is today owned by the Science Museum in London. It is the oldest patent motor car in original condition that is known to exist.

Emile Roger died prematurely at his father's house in Châteauvillain in 1897, two months after having suffered a cerebral stroke that caused a general paralysis.

Roger engaged in many races to promote the reliability and efficacy of the Roger Benz automobile.

In 1897, the time of restraint was over. Despite having the new planetary gearbox, which after all had three speeds, their motor cars could hardly manage even relatively modest inclines. As a result, the sales of the Victoria and its fellow models were in decline, whereas up to this point they had controlled the European market.

In 1896, Benz established a dedicated department of motor vehicle engine design at his Mannheim company and set about developing efficient multi-cylinder engines. His first design in 1897 resulted in the prototype for a 2-cylinder unit, with cylinders coupled in parallel. This 'twin engine' was like the in-line engines being developed by other manufacturers of the day.

Benz & Cie and its new engine department continued to be ahead of their time in virtually every part of the industry, and it was not long before a new engine concept was announced in which the cylinders were positioned in an arrangement opposing one another. This arrangement found application in passenger cars, commercial vehicles and racing cars.

This new drive concept offered several advantages over in-line engines. Above all, with the cylinders set at 180 degrees to one another, dynamic masses were much better balanced, since the timing of the pistons in such an opposed configuration meant that any momentum produced by the

Benz chose the name 'Contra-Motor' for his engine with horizontally positioned cylinders because the pistons, although attached to the same crankshaft, worked in contrary motion.

power/intake strokes and the exhaust/compression strokes was effectively counterbalanced by the corresponding piston movement of the opposite side. This piston movement was possible thanks to a double-offset crankshaft, which meant the two cylinders were slightly offset within the open-topped engine frame. This configuration also allowed for a compact and flat design of the boxer engine.

Over the next two years. Benz's engineers developed this so-called 'contra engine' to production standard and, as early as 1898, were installing a 4.2-litre variant in buses. The fully matured 1.7-litre and 2.7-litre engines, with outputs of 5hp (4kW) and 8hp (5.9kW) respectively, finally made their debut in the Benz Dos-à-Dos of 1899.

The natural balance of the opposed cylinders allowed a smaller flywheel to be fitted and permitted higher revs. Benz mated the engine to a three-speed planetary transmission, running the rear wheels via a pair of chains, which enabled his horseless carriage to achieve a top speed of approximately 30km/h (19mph). With the greater pulling power of the Contra-Motor, there was less need for shifting and therefore less work for the driver.

Power output was increased steadily. Whereas the 5hp engine of the Dos-à-Dos initially remained unmodified, the larger variant with a displacement of 2690cc initially delivered 8hp (5.9kW) in 1899, then

The original 2-cylinder opposed engine design by Hoch and Benz.

Driver and front passenger sat back to back with the other passengers in the Benz Dos-à-Dos, the model that celebrated its premiere with the contra engine in 1899.

9hp (6.6kW) in 1900 and finally 10hp (7.4kW) in 1901. By 1902, with an increased engine speed of 980rpm instead of 920rpm, the tried-and-tested engine finally achieved 12hp (8.8kW).

Production of this engine was discontinued in 1900, but in 1902 the aforementioned Benz Ideal was also offered with a contra engine with 2090cc displacement and an output of 8hp (5.9kW) at 1,000rpm. Predecessor models of the Ideal were still equipped with a single-cylinder engine.

The new engine also proved itself on the racetrack. The brand's first-ever vehicle built specifically for motor sport competition was the 8hp Benz racing car introduced in 1899; this was later upgraded to 12hp. There was also a 4-cylinder racing version of the boxer with a 5440cc displacement developed by Georg Diehl.

The era of Benz's contra engine finally came to an end in 1902, when it was replaced by the twin-cylinder engine. It was also developed into an in-line 4-cylinder version.

The boxer engine not only enjoyed success in passenger cars but also commercial vehicles such as this passenger 'bus'.

With the contra engine to victory: Fritz Held and navigator Hans Thum at the wheel of an 8hp Benz racing car, after taking victory at the Frankfurt–Cologne long-distance car race on 2 January 1899.

THE FIRST COUPÉ MOTOR CAR: THE MYLORD

Although the Benz Dos-à-Dos-style Mylord Coupé still did not manage to shake its horse carriage past, it was the motorized coupé that begat them all.

Similar in style to the brougham carriages, the Mylord's coachman sat in the front, while the driver, a 'liveried' chauf-feur, was placed in front and, in most instances, in the open, exposed to the elements while rear passengers could sit protected in comfort under a solid bodyshell.

Also like the brougham 'cut' carriage, the door was positioned at the lowest part of the underbody with a low-slung footstep to enable easy mounting and alighting. This blended seamlessly into wheel mudguards.

The Mylord Coupé was introduced to the line at about

The Mylord featured a collapsible landaulet rear roof section that allowed passengers to enjoy the day if the weather was pleasant, while the rather elaborate side windows could be lowered and folded to permit even further ventilation.

More than most any other body style of its period, the Mylord was reminiscent of a horse-drawn carriage that had lost its horse: without the pneumatic tyres and vertically mounted steering wheel, it resembled a brougham.

BENZ MYLORD COUPÉ SPECIFICATION

Engine	Rear mounted, four-stroke, two opposed cylinders (Contra-Motor)
Bore × stroke	120×120mm
Total displacement	2690cc
Gearing	Three forward gears, one reverse gear
Maximum speed	35–40km/h (21–25mph)
Rated output	10hp at 920rpm
Drivetrain	Flat belt on intermediate gearbox; chains on rear wheels
Length	3,300mm (130in)
Width	1,850mm (73in)
Height	2,200mm (87in)
Kerb weight	650–1,300kg (1,433–2,866lb), depending on version
Price	RM 3,800–7,800, depending on the model

the same time that the Contra-Motor was introduced. Estimates of production numbers for the Mylord Coupé design vary; reportedly all were for sale in the United Kingdom by Emile Roger, and allegedly even used by the British royal family.

THE BENZ PARSIFAL

Up to 1900, Benz was selling more than 600 vehicles a year and had become one of the largest automobile manufacturers in Europe. In 1901, however, the number fell to 385 and in 1902 to just 226. Much of this decline was due to Benz remaining faithful to already outdated designs, but it was also caused partly by the sales success of the Mercedes.

The design manager and commercial director of the Benz company, Julius Ganss, strongly recommended a modernization of the range of products, and to this end encouraged Frenchman Marius Barbarou into his development team. Barbarou had previously run his own 'French' design office with five colleagues, where he further developed the plans for cars and engines that he had brought with him from his home country. At the same time, the 'German' design office under Diehl and Erle was developing a completely new series of engines.

The new Parsifal series ultimately combined the French

In December 1902, the 10/12 HP Benz Parsifal was presented to an international audience at the fifth Paris Motor Show.

The later Benz Parsifal type 24/40 HP landaulet of 1906.

BENZ 16/50HP SPECIFICATION

Engine	Front mounted, four-stroke, six in-line cylinders (two groups of three)
Bore × stroke	80 × 138mm
Total displacement	4160cc
Gearing	Four-speed manual
Maximum speed	90km/h (56mph)
Rated output	50hp at 2,000rpm
Drivetrain	Cardan driveshafts to rear wheels
Length	4,800mm (189in)
Width	1,830mm (72in)
Height	1,950mm (77in)
Kerb weight	1,750kg (3,858lb)
Price	RM 12,000–19,500 (1923–1927)

**In little over fifteen years, the carriage style was replaced by elegant
shapes, although still retaining cabriolet design.**

vehicle designs with the German engines, as they had proven
to be better than the French ones, but Benz was not really
satisfied with this solution. Interdepartmental bickering
ensued, with neither of the two competing departments
asserting itself. Karl Benz, also dissatisfied, could not get
over the fact that Barbarou was now identified as the leading engineer in the development of the new cars and so left
the management in April 1903. Barbarou, for his part, was
offended that his engine designs were discarded and said
goodbye in the autumn of the same year, with Julius Ganss
following six months later.

Against all the odds, the new model series was eventually
launched at the start of 1903 under the designation Parsifal.
It comprised three 2-cylinder models with Cardan drive (8,
10, and 12hp), as well as a 16hp 4-cylinder model with chain
drive.

The most important part of this story is that this vehicle
at last did away with its 'carriage' heritage, mainly due to
the larger engines sitting upright and so having to be
placed at the front of the vehicle under a cowling. This
subsequently became the shape of every automobile after
it.

THE BENZ 16/50 HP

Just as the Mylord Coupé was not strictly a coupé, neither
is the Benz 16/50 HP; however, it is included in this book as
it shows the progress of Benz design as we approach what
became the saloon coupé-style body.

In the early days of motoring, closed saloons were the
exception rather than the rule. Indeed, until well into the

1930s, manufacturers and buyers more often went for open variants, particularly where more exclusive models were concerned, so it was almost inevitable that a coupé-style body would derive from a cabriolet. The 16/50 HP had a two-door roadster body style with a front-positioned engine supplying power to the rear wheels.

This was one of the most important models in the Benz car range running up to the merger with the Daimler-Motoren-Gesellschaft in 1926. After the fusion of Benz and Daimler to form Daimler-Benz AG, it was offered under the name Mercedes-Benz 16/50 HP and continued in production until 1927.

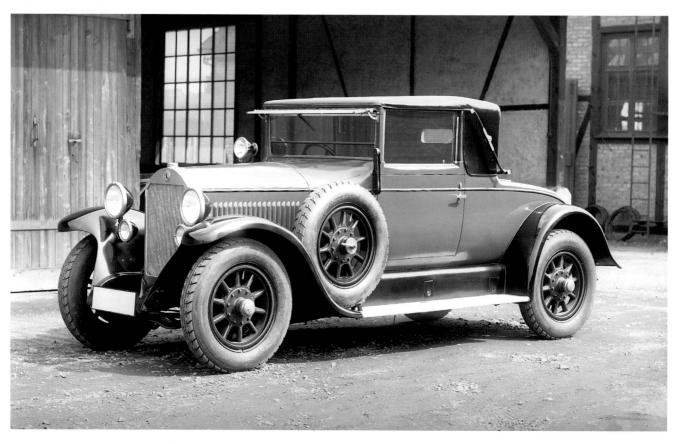

The sports cabriolet design was the forerunner of the coupé.

CHAPTER FIVE

PRE-MERGER DAIMLER

Daimler's 'motor carriage' was the first four-wheel vehicle driven by a high-speed combustion engine. Contrary to the Benz patent motor car, which boasted an independent integral construction, Daimler's first automobile was merely a carriage without shaft and with the common fifth-wheel steering: a carriage without horses, so to speak.

Daimler and Maybach knew their strengths lay in their engine, and so for the time being neither thought that an evolution model or even the series production of Daimler's motor vehicle would follow. All they really wanted to do was to demonstrate the possible ways of using his engine, and accordingly they carried on looking for alternatives.

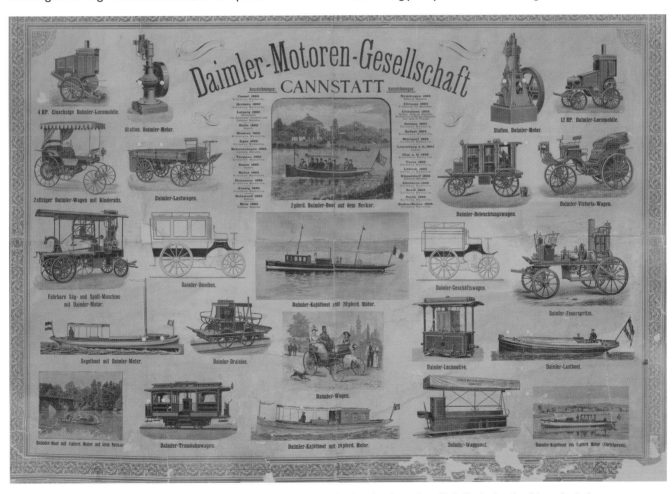

The Daimler product range from 1896. From the beginning, Gottlieb Daimler had in mind that his engines should be used as universally as possible. He kept coming up with new ways to drive vehicles, boats, pumps or dynamos, as the building programme from 1896 shows.

In 1889, Maybach constructed the elegant, lightweight and technically advanced Daimler wire-wheeled car as a complete automobile. It was equipped with a 2-cylinder V engine, water-cooled cylinder heads, a pipe cooling circuit, hot tube ignition, float-type carburettor, and the world's first four-speed gearwheel transmission, though still without double-pivot steering.

A modified version of the wire-wheel car was sold by DMG in the years from 1892 to 1895 as the 'Daimler Motorwagen'. It was created, however, without the involvement of Daimler and Maybach. Max Schroedter, the new technical director of DMG, was responsible for the modified variation – which, incidentally, was no longer fitted with steel wheels.

In 1889, both Daimler and Maybach succumbed to pressure to build a stand-alone automobile in the shape of what has come to be known as the 'Daimler wire-wheeled car', realizing – as Benz did – that the way forward would be development on the bicycle theme. Presented at the Paris World Exhibition in 1889, the wire-wheeled car was in a way the impetus for the setting up of the French automobile industry. The first motor cars constructed in France were made at Peugeot in 1890 and at Panhard & Levassor in the middle of 1891. Each company used Daimler engines, which had been built under licence at Panhard & Levassor since the end of 1889.

In contrast to the original Daimler motor carriage, the wire-wheel car, now with upright 2-cylinder engine, a 4-speed toothed-wheel gearbox and the axle-pivot steering, represented a huge leap forward in the construction of a real stand-alone automobile.

Having left DMG following disagreements, Maybach and Daimler, together with twelve workers, returned to the former Hotel Hermann in Cannstatt and, along with five apprentices, continued their design work on both engines and engine applications; the result was the 'Riemenwagen' (belt-driven car), a carriage-like automobile.

Its newly developed rear-mounted 'Phoenix' engine featured two jointed block-cast, parallel-standing cylinders and a camshaft for controlling the exhaust valves, as well as a flywheel cooling system. Its power was transmitted to the rear wheels by a belt system. Also new was the spray nozzle carburettor, the forefather of the modern carburettor, which was developed by Maybach.

The Daimler four-gear belt transmission Riemenwagen of 1895.

The Riemenwagen has a firm place in history for Daimler for a number of reasons: the first motorized taxi in the world was a Daimler Riemenwagen, the world's first motorized truck used the Phoenix engine, and the Riemenwagen was the beginning of the relationship with Emil Jellinek.

It was also a Riemenwagen that Daimler and Maybach used during their tests on electric ignition, which Benz – at that time a competitor – had used in his vehicles right from the start. In July, an 8hp car equipped with a Bosch low-voltage magnetic ignition was driven by Otto Salzer on a five-day test drive through the Austrian Alps. Due to the experience gained on this trip, the hot-tube ignition system that was characteristic of Daimler engine construction was soon replaced. In 1897, DMG introduced a new generation of motor cars, which were the first Daimler automobiles to feature a front-mounted engine. These represented the first important step away from the belt-driven motor carriage to the modern automobile.

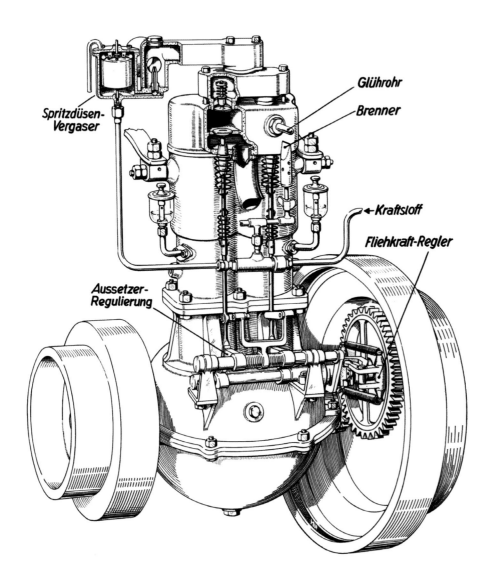

Spritzdüsen-Vergaser

Glührohr

Brenner

Kraftsloff

Fliehkraft-Regler

Aussetzer-Regulierung

The first 2-cylinder Daimler Phoenix engine, 1895–9.

The failure of the aforementioned Max Schroedter-designed 'Daimler Motorwagen' of 1892 to 1895 almost bankrupted DMG, which led to both Daimler and Maybach returning to the company. They immediately set about producing a revised belt-driven car using various models of the Phoenix 2-cylinder engine: from the 2hp version with 750cc displacement, and the 3, 4 and 6hp varieties, to the 2.2-litre engine, with 7.5–8hp. All together, around 150 units of the belt-driven car, which was officially known as the 'Daimler-Motor-Kutsche' (Daimler motor carriage) were produced, the majority of them with 4hp engines.

NICE WEEK AND THE MERCEDES 35 HP

Emil Jellinek had been present at the Nice Week speed trials in March 1900, when a Daimler works driver, Wilhelm Bauer, suffered fatal injuries when his short-wheelbase Daimler Phoenix failed to negotiate the first turn of the

Here (top right) Gottlieb Daimler, his closest colleague, Wilhelm Maybach, and Meister Bauer presented the 5-ton truck with a 2-cylinder Phoenix engine. Bottom: The first Daimler 4hp truck with a 1,500kg (3,300lb) payload, 1896.

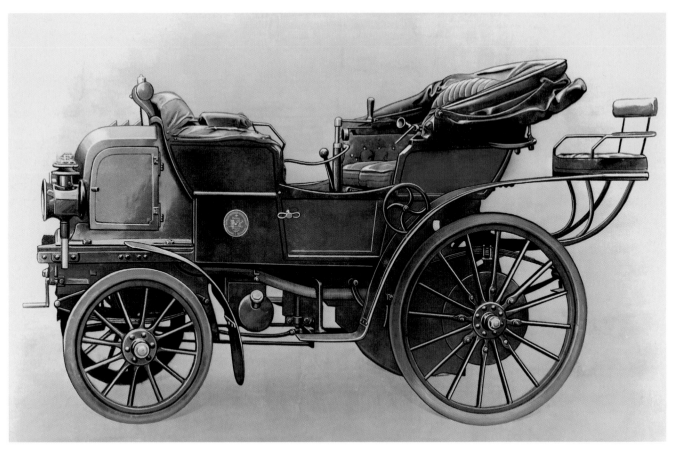

ABOVE: **The Daimler Vis-à-Vis with a 6hp, 2-cylinder Phoenix engine, from the year 1897. The engine was transposed to the front for the first time.**

The Nice–La Turbie hill climb, 3 March 1900: the site of the crash that killed **Wilhelm Bauer** in the 23hp Daimler Phoenix racing car.

The all-new 35hp 4-cylinder engine.

The Mercedes 35 HP, the first modern automobile, 1901.

The long-wheelbase version of the 35 HP.

EMIL JELLINEK

Born: 6 April 1853, Leipzig, Germany
Died: 21 January 1918, Geneva, Switzerland

The successful businessman and automobile enthusiast Emil Jellinek came from a family of scholars. He was born the second son of Leipzig rabbi and later chief rabbi of Vienna, Adolf Jellinek, and his wife, Rosalie. He had two brothers.

In contrast to his father and brothers, Emil Jellinek failed to develop an interest in theology, law or philology. Following instead in the footsteps of his uncle, Moritz Jellinek, who had established the Budapest Tram Company, he joined the Imperial Royal Privileged Austrian North-Western Railway Company.

His eager interest in engineering and technology took him from the bicycle to the automobile and, after gaining his first experience of automobiles with vehicles from De Dion-Bouton and Léon Bollée, he purchased for himself a Benz Victoria.

The motor car concept was still in its infancy and a somewhat costly pursuit, but his successful insurance and stock dealings provided the necessary capital to fund his preoccupation with the automobile.

After his father arranged a position for him as secretary to the Austro-Hungarian consul, Erwin A. Schmidl, Jellinek left the railway company to focus on a diplomatic career. In 1874, he became vice-consul in Algeria and an agent for a French insurance company in Algiers and Vienna. His gift for languages stood him in good stead in all these fields of work – he spoke perfect

Emil Jellinek.

Jellinek went from a deep interest in the bicycle to buying a Benz Victoria.

French and Spanish as well as German.

Seeing an advertisement for a DMG car in the weekly magazine *Fliegende Blätter* (Flying Pages), Jellinek, now forty-three, travelled to Cannstatt in 1896 to find out more about the company, its factory and the designers Gottlieb Daimler and Wilhelm Maybach. He placed an order for one of the Daimler cars and took delivery in October of that year.

The car, a Phoenix double phaeton with 6hp engine, could reach 24km/h (15mph). Maybach had designed the DMG Phoenix engine, which featured four cylinders for the first time in a car.

DMG seemed a reliable enterprise, so Jellinek decided to start selling its cars. In 1898, he wrote to DMG requesting six more cars and to become a DMG main agent and distributor. In 1899 he sold ten cars and in 1900 twenty-nine. Among French carmakers such as Peugeot, Panhard & Levassor, as well as other makers licensed to sell Daimler-engined vehicles in France, there was a shortage of cars, and Jellinek benefited by being able to beat other suppliers' lengthy waiting times.

Emil Jellinek and his chauffeur, Hermann Braun, in Baden near Vienna with his first Daimler vehicle – the 6hp Phoenix double phaeton model from 1898 – which he had purchased in Cannstatt.

Jellinek demanded ever faster and more powerful cars from DMG and entered these in race meetings, the most important of these being the Nice Week in the south of France, where he would race under a pseudonym. He used the first name of his daughter from his first marriage, Mercédès, born in 1889, a name that was soon commonly heard in motoring circles. Jellinek's orders accounted for an ever-increasing share of the company's total output: in 1898 he ordered three out of a total of fifty-seven vehicles, rising to ten out of 108 in 1899 and twenty-eight out of ninety-six by 1900.

In April 1900, when Jellinek and DMG made an agreement about the sale of cars and engines, the name was also included as a product designation. Above all, it was decided that a new engine would be developed that would 'bear the name Daimler-Mercedes'. A mere fourteen days later, Jellinek ordered thirty-six vehicles totalling 550,000 marks – a truly huge order for the time. Several weeks later, he placed a new order for another thirty-six vehicles, all with 8hp engines.

His key sales terrain was the French Riviera, which Jellinek was quick to recognize as a perfect location for his business activities, as it was here that the high society of Europe (and elsewhere) gathered, particularly in the winter. Well-connected Jellinek had an important influencing role in DMG business policy: without his dogged insistence, the company would most likely have withdrawn from motor racing in 1900, in the wake of Wilhelm Bauer's accident. Instead, the innovative Mercedes 35 HP was developed.

From the present-day point of view, like Emile Roger for Benz, Jellinek can be seen as a highly gifted marketing specialist.

Emil Jellinek at the wheel of his Daimler 16hp Phoenix racing car, next to Hermann Braun. On the back seat, from left to right: Ferdinand Spiegel, Otto Zels and Ferdinand Jellinek.

His success and the major orders that he placed in the spring of 1900 for a total of seventy-two vehicles earned him a seat on DMG's supervisory board. In this position, he made the case for the catchy product name 'Mercedes', which he regarded as having the potential to make an international impact. On 23 June 1902, the name was duly announced as a trademark and was legally registered on 26 September.

Having been used as Jellinek's racing pseudonym, the name 'Mercedes' was announced as a trademark and became the name of every Daimler car henceforth.

In June 1903, in an unusual twist, Emil Jellinek legally changed his own name to Jellinek-Mercedes, commenting that it was probably the first time in history that a man has taken the name of his daughter.

At the end of 1904, sales activities for the Mercedes automobile, which had been dominated by Jellinek up to this point, were placed on a broader footing with the establishment of the Mercédès Société Française d'Automobiles. This new sales company, in which Jellinek and DMG held an interest, took over Jellinek's sales and distribution rights for the Mercedes automobiles at the beginning of 1906. In the same year, Jellinek and DMG established a further joint company in the guise of the Société des Automobiles Commerciales, which took over the plant of the Austrian Daimler-Motoren-Gesellschaft in Wiener Neustadt.

In 1908, Jellinek withdrew from the automobile business to focus more upon his diplomatic duties as the consul of the United States of Mexico in Nice – a post he had held since 1904. In 1908, he became honorary consul in Monaco, and in 1909 director of the Austro-Hungarian consulate in Monaco. After the outbreak of World War I, Jellinek (in France) and his wife (in Austria) were suspected of espionage by people with grudges to bear. This prompted the family to retire to Geneva, where Emil Jellinek died in 1918.

PAUL DAIMLER

Born: 13 September 1869, Karlsruhe, Germany
Died: 15 December 1945, Berlin, Germany

Paul Daimler, the eldest son of the company founder, worked in the design office of Daimler-Motoren-Gesellschaft (DMG) from 1897 onwards. Having clashed with Wilhelm Maybach on a number of occasions, however, Daimler junior was given his own independent design office and soon began designing a small car of his own. Having spent his formative years around Panhard & Levassor he was aware that the small cars known as voiturettes in France had become highly popular, and sensed that it would be possible to gain access to this market segment with a modern DMG design.

Paul Daimler.

The young Daimler brother often considered Wilhelm Maybach's design concepts as competition to his own and was not best pleased that Daimler senior overruled him, insisting that his time would be better spent assisting them in finishing the Mercedes 35 HP.

Undeterred, four months later, at the end of October, Paul Daimler eventually returned to and completed the draft of his own version of the 'first modern automobile' so that the drawings could be passed on to the workshop, which was to start building three prototypes.

In March 1903, the 'Paul Daimler lightweight car' was presented in a modified version as a coupé and double phaeton at the International Automobile Exhibition in Vienna. In spite of his highly modern designs, however, none of the Paul Daimler cars went into mass production: on the one hand, they would have been over-attractive competition to the Mercedes models designed by Maybach, and on the other the sales success of the Mercedes kept DMG production stretched to its full capacity. What the cars did do, alongside the Maybach/Mercedes, was to show that design was not just about function but had the ability to introduce innovation and identity.

Daimler junior went on to develop some excellent engineering strategies, especially after his father died. He and Maybach eventually managed to work alongside and support one another, even under strain of the DMG board.

Ultimately, the Paul Daimler model should be recognized as the 'father of the modern car in shape and design'.

The Paul Daimler wagon with its tonneau cover raised.

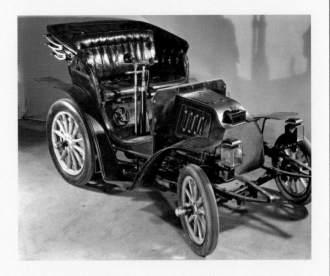

The Paul Daimler wagon in open-air form.

hill climb to La Turbie from Nice. Bauer's car struck the outer wall head on. While his passenger, Hermann Braun, survived, Bauer died the next day.

Learning from this tragedy, Jellinek pointed out to Daimler engineer Maybach that 'the French appreciated long ago that to be stable a racing car must be low, wide, and long'. This was also evident to Maybach, but Jellinek's urging reinforced the direction he was taking. In February1900, Maybach had already started work on a more powerful engine for the first Mercedes. Sadly, on 6 March of that year, he suffered the loss of his mentor Daimler, already ill from overwork. Duttenhofer was now in sole charge at Daimler.

On those spring days back in 1901, the powerful sound of the four cylinders heralded the future: the Mercedes 35 HP built by Daimler-Motoren-Gesellschaft (DMG) in Cannstatt appeared able to control at will the diverse competitions of the Nice Week motorsport event.

'The French design engineers clearly have nothing to challenge it,' wrote *La Presse* newspaper on 30 March 1901, after the third win for Mercedes in the space of as many days.

Paul Meyan, the founding member and secretary-general of the Automobile Club de France (ACF), is on record as having said about the Mercedes 35 HP: 'With this passion for innovation, visionary drive and technical creativity, we have entered the Mercedes era.'

The Mercedes 35 HP was the first Mercedes that was no longer reminiscent of a carriage pulled along by a combustion engine instead of horses. Its totally new construction was designed for performance, weight saving and safety, its key features being a lightweight high-performance engine, a long wheelbase and a low centre of gravity. With these attributes and the honeycomb radiator organically integrated into the front, it gave the automobile its own distinct form for the first time.

Experts were immediately aware that this vehicle marked a profound change in the field of automotive engineering.

The Mercedes Simplex was produced in 20, 30 and 40 HP variants.

The Mercedes Simplex's engine was mounted over the front axle. The engine's power was taken from a sprocket flywheel, 600mm (24in) in diameter, transmitting to the rear drive by a long roller chain.

THE MERCEDES SIMPLEX, 1902

The Mercedes 35 HP and its less powerful sister models, the 12/16 HP and the 8/11 HP, gave rise in 1902 to the Mercedes Simplex model family, which initially comprised three models. The 'Simplex' designation alluded to the vehicles' ease of operation by the standards of the day. The most powerful variant in 1902 was the Mercedes Simplex 40 HP, the direct successor to the Mercedes 35 HP.

The Simplex vehicles were equally successful as innovative racing cars and as sporty everyday luxury automobiles. Both the 40 HP and the 28 HP versions dominated Nice Week in April 1902, even more than the first Mercedes had done the previous year. E.T. Stead was victorious in the La Turbie

hill climb race, achieving an even higher average speed of 55.2km/h (34.3mph).

The Mercedes Simplex laid the foundation of a new car category, the super-luxury class: with an imposing touring saloon body, it was unlike anything else on the market at the time and quickly established itself with royalty and aristocrats. Its immense size and luxuries were to set the benchmark for the development of this 'Sonderklasse' (special class), with the S-Class model continuing for a century.

In 1902, Maybach decided to incorporate a series of modifications to the Simplex, anticipating many sales around the French Riviera, where Jellinek based his agency. To suit their predominantly high-society clients, the new Mercedes would be shown publicly, not on a platform or static in a show, but

The 28/32 'open-air touring car' (Tourenwagen) was offered for the first time in a production car with the V-shaped radiator grille later reserved for 6-cylinder or racing cars.

'while driving through the most traditional avenues in town or to picnic in a park'.

The Simplex's engine was mounted over the front axle. The engine's power was taken from a sprocket flywheel, 60cm (24in) in diameter, transmitting it to the rear drive by a long roller chain. The gate-gear manual gearbox featured four speeds and reverse, controlling a coil spring clutch acting on the flywheel system. A lever produced both declutching and deceleration together.

Both axles were rigid, featuring semi-elliptic springs. The steering axles were located at the extremes, decreasing the transmission of road shocks to the driver's hands. Originally the wheels were wooden, with twelve non-removable spokes and pneumatic tyres. Later, in 1905, the Mercedes Simplex pioneered cast-steel wheels and, for the first time, acquired an innovative, powerful twin-brake system, one operated by hand and the other by foot. The main handbrake acted on the rear wheels with drum brakes, while

the secondary foot brake acted on the chain drive's intermediate driveshaft; both systems were water-cooled by a sprinkling system over hot zones when braking.

The body itself was offered in a number of configurations: a large Berlin with an enclosed passenger area, a simpler tonneau version, an open-air Tourenwagen and a coupé.

The Simplex Coupé

The Simplex Coupé was a true coupé in the carriage style, with a plushily appointed rear passenger area that was completely enclosed. It was separated from the driver by a glass bulkhead. The driver was semi-protected by an overhanging roof although the side were open.

Unusually there were three mudguards on each side, one over each of the wheels and a central one to keep any dirt or water from the step to the passenger cubicle.

The 4-cylinder engine was completely covered in a cowling and cooled by the Maybach radiator.

Mercedes Simplex 'Coupé-Karosserie'.

The Simplex continued in production until 1910 with many improvements. The introduction of a luxury tax in July 1906 led to an agreement in 1909 between all manufacturers that were members of the German Motor Vehicle Manufactur-

ers' Association (VDMI) to use the displacement-related tax category as part of the model designation. Thus from 1905, the word 'Simplex' was omitted from the model designation and just the hp designation was used, then, as per the agreement, DMG adjusted the model designations in 1909, converting the 45 HP into the 26/45 HP, for instance, and the 65 HP into the 36/65 HP.

MERCEDES SIMPLEX SPECIFICATION

Engine	Front-mounted, four-stroke, four in-line cylinders (two groups of two)
Bore × stroke	110 × 140mm
Total displacement	5315cc
Gearing	Four-speed manual
Maximum speed	60km/h (37mph)
Rated output	32hp at 1,200rpm
Drivetrain	Chain to rear wheels
Wheelbase	2,400mm (94in)
Front/rear track	1,420mm (56in)
Height	1,950mm (77in)
Kerb weight	1,250kg (2,756lb)
Price	Mk 20,000–24,000 (option dependent)

The 4-cylinder Simplex engine.

MERCEDES 37/90 HP AND 38/100 HP, 1911–15

In June 1911, the Mercedes 37/90 HP was introduced as the new top model in the DMG sales range. The new high-performance car, whose 4-cylinder engine was equipped with three-valve technology and dual ignition, replaced the 6-cylinder models that had been built since 1907 and, like these, was chain-driven. The 37/90 HP was the last new development of Daimler-Motoren-Gesellschaft to come onto the market with chain drive. A special new feature was the encapsulation of the drive chains, which were running in an oil bath.

The 9.5-litre engine designed by Paul Daimler had an especially large intake valve and two smaller exhaust valves for each cylinder. The valve arrangement in the cylinder head

The Mercedes 37/90 HP sport cabriolet.

The Mercedes 37/90 HP sport phaeton.

This was also one of the first production Mercedes models available with a pointed radiator.

permitted short gas cycles and, as a result, efficient combustion. The valves were operated via pushrods and rocker arms by a lateral cam-shaft, driven by toothed gears from the centre of the crankshaft. Halfway through 1913, the 37/90 HP, like the other models in the range, was given a new model designation, becoming the 37/95 HP. One and a half years later, the displacement was raised to 9.8 litres and the model designation was changed once more to 38/100 HP.

Although this top model of the DMG range was neither a racing car nor a typical coupé, it shows how DMG changed the design of a single model to meet customer desires. The sport phaeton was a case in point: minus its top and with its windscreen removed, it was a sporting grand tourer, but return the screen and put up the tonneau roof and it was a limousine again. It is included here as the creation of a sporty, powerful touring car of the most advanced design marked a change in company policy, and laid the foundations of what became the coupé concept.

In 1922, Paul Daimler was intent on developing a new 8-cylinder model, but the DMG supervisory board wanted him to come up with something a little more readily market-able as a mass-production car; the resulting disagreement led him to leave the company his father had founded and join the automobile manufacturer Horch in Zwickau, where he was able to realize his 8-cylinder project. His succes-sor, Ferdinand Porsche, became head of the design office on 30 April 1923. This was not the first time Porsche had

followed in the footsteps of Paul Daimler – seventeen years previously he had succeeded Daimler as technical director at DMG's Austrian subsidiary in Wiener Neustadt.

FERDINAND PORSCHE AT THE HELM

Although sticking with the supercharger technology that had been introduced by Paul Daimler, Porsche set about developing two new racing cars as well as two high-end passenger car models. In 1924, DMG embarked on a joint venture with their engineering rivals Benz & Cie, and it was mainly due to this union that the new chief designer's efforts bore its first fruits.

The Mercedes 2-litre 'Targa Florio' supercharged racing car, 1924. It was in this car that Christian Werner won the Targa Florio and Coppa Florio in 1924 (below).

The 2-litre 4-cylinder racer developed from the previous year's Indianapolis car under Porsche's direction won Sicily's demanding Targa Florio with Christian Werner at the wheel. Sadly there was a less felicitous outcome for the newly designed 2-litre 8-cylinder racer on its first outing at the Italian Grand Prix in Monza: Count Zborowski left the track having suffered fatal injuries. Race director Max Sailer immediately pulled the other two Mercedes out of the race. For the 1925 race season, however, the 8-cylinder racing car was once again to achieve considerable success.

Although the 15/70/100 HP and 24/100/140 HP models were exactly midway between the two racing cars in terms of number of cylinders, their respective displacements (4.0 and 6.3 litres) were in both cases significantly higher. As was common practice at that time, the model designations were made up of a first number, which stood for 'fiscal horsepower' (based on engine displacement), and a second number that represented the effective engine power. A third number applied exclusively to supercharged vehicles, denoting the power delivered by the engine with the supercharger in operation.

In terms of technical design, the two 6-cylinder models were broadly identical. Apart from the engine, the only differences related to the wheelbase, overall length and some bodywork details. Just like the 6/25 HP and 10/40 HP 4-cylinder models unveiled by DMG at the end of 1921 as the company's first series-produced supercharged passenger cars, the two 6-cylinder supercharged vehicles were also powered by engines of exceptionally modern design. Although, as in the 4-cylinder models, the overhead camshaft was driven by a vertical shaft, it was housed inside a removable cast-iron cylinder head. Similarly, cast iron was the material of choice for the cylinder liners, which were fitted into the light-alloy engine block, in contrast to the individually machined steel cylinders that were welded to the cylinder head on the 4-cylinder models,

Porsche's success with the supercharged engined race cars spilled over into the production of his newly designed passenger automobiles – after all, his designs were built with mass production in mind. They also played a key part in the restructuring of the production programme, a task DMG had embarked upon even before entering into its alliance with Benz & Cie. This standardization and modernization of the product range took on an even greater importance in the context of the Daimler-Benz joint venture and was expedited with top priority from the very beginning.

Alongside the two luxury-class automobiles, Porsche's department in Stuttgart was also developing a 2-litre model that, although designed according to similar principles, was not yet so far advanced. Its high production costs meant that the technically sophisticated design was not entirely suitable for a low-cost mass-produced vehicle. At the end of a long and protracted debate conducted at numerous board meetings, the Mannheim contingent succeeded in forcing through their ideas and in launching the design of a less ambitious, reliable, and cheap-to-produce model. In late 1926, it was not Porsche's two-litre supercharged model, but the 8/38 HP and 12/55 HP that went into production.

At the Daimler-Motoren-Gesellschaft factory in Untertürkheim, the Mercedes team got together for a photograph prior to departure for the 1924 Targa Florio. At the wheel of the supercharged 120hp 2-litre 4-cylinder Mercedes Targa Florio race cars were (from left) Max Sailer, Christian Werner, Alfred Neubauer and Christian Lautenschlager. Otto Salzer (far right) drove a Mercedes Targa Florio chassis race car with a modified 4.5-litre Grand Prix engine (the 'Grandmother') from 1914. Wings and registration plates were added for the road journey to the race venue.

The 1924 Mercedes 2.0-litre racing motor type M7294, the 'Targa Florio'.

© Mercedes-Benz AG

Although generally only referred to as the four-door or the two-door 8/38, it became an official saloon coupé.

The supercharged Mercedes 24/100/140 HP Pullman limousine of 1924 epitomized the desire for luxury.

MERCEDES 15/70/100 HP AND 24/110/140 HP MODEL K, 1924–30

The two 6-cylinder supercharged models made their debut in December 1924 at the German Motor Show in Berlin, which celebrated its twenty-fifth anniversary by inaugurating an additional exhibition hall. Although originally scheduled for September, the car show had been postponed by two months on account of the unfavourable economic situation. Having already gone into production in July and September, some of the new Mercedes models were on show in Mercedes sales rooms as early as October.

Both models were available in a variety of body versions. The choice included open tourers in five- or seven-seater variants, a seven-seater Pullman saloon and of course a six-seater coupé touring saloon. The two tourers were also optionally available with a removable Pullman top. The most expensive version was the Pullman saloon at a price of 22,750 Reichsmark for the 15/70/100 HP and RM 27,750 for the 24/100/140 HP.

By December 1924, production of all other Mercedes passenger car models had come to an end with only two units of the Mercedes Knight 16/50 HP being built in January 1925. This meant that, from February 1925 onwards,

the two 6-cylinder supercharged models were Mercedes' only contribution to the joint venture's passenger car sales programme. Benz & Cie augmented the line-up with three passenger car models of their own that covered the mid-range segment, but, as older models, they were unable to offer the latest available technology.

An early piece of publicity advertising the new Coupé de Ville based on the 24/100/140 HP.

There was, therefore, a serious need to renew the mid-range product line-up, something which did not happen until October 1926. That month saw the launch of the 8/38 HP and 12/55 HP under the new brand name of Mercedes-Benz, the joint-venture partners having merged in June of that year to form Daimler-Benz AG. From then on, the new marque was applied also to the previously launched Mercedes and Benz models in the sales programme.

The names of the two 6-cylinder supercharged models included the additions 'R litre' and 'S litre', something that led to frequent confusion in the case of the top-of-the-line model, which had a displacement of 6.3 litres from the outset. Even more confusing was the fact that some in-house documents also referred to it as the '600 model'.

Mercedes 24/100/140 HP Coupé W9456

This series was built between 1924 and 1929. It came to embody the ideal of a 'big Mercedes' in the 1920s. The 6-cylinder supercharged cars launched in 1924 occupied a special place in the product history of the Mercedes and Mercedes-Benz brands, and it is often forgotten that not only did they pave the way for supercharger technology to finally make its breakthrough into series production, but they formed the design basis for the legendary 'S' series models. These in turn became the basis for further evolutions up to the legendary SSKL and did more than any other model series to shape the image of the new brand with the star.

The Mercedes 24/100/140 HP became the new flagship model in the passenger car range, taking over from the 28/95 HP, which had been discontinued in August 1924.

To meet the needs of performance-minded customers, a sporty version of the 24/100/140 HP was developed in early 1926 in the run-up to the merger. This evolutionary version had a reduced-length chassis with a 350mm shorter wheelbase and was named the 'K' model, the 'K' standing for 'kurzer Radstand' (short wheelbase). Apart from the shorter length, the vehicle also featured a technical modification to the rear axle, with the cantilever half-springs on the basic version being replaced on the K by conventional underslung half-springs. The engine included additional modifications: the compression ratio was raised to 5.0 and the high-voltage magneto ignition was augmented by battery ignition, which supplied a second set of spark plugs.

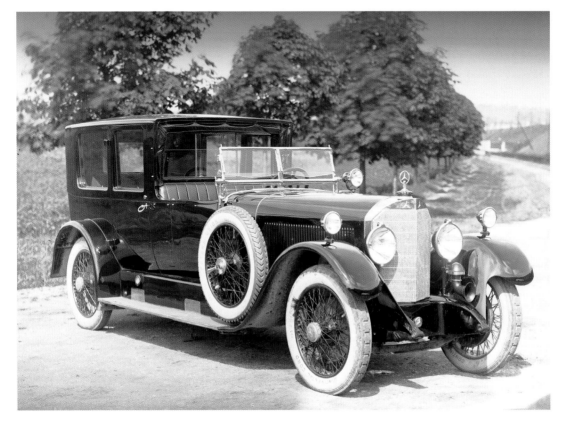

The Pullman city coupé, also known as the Coupé de Ville, had a strengthened, fixed roof section for storing luggage.

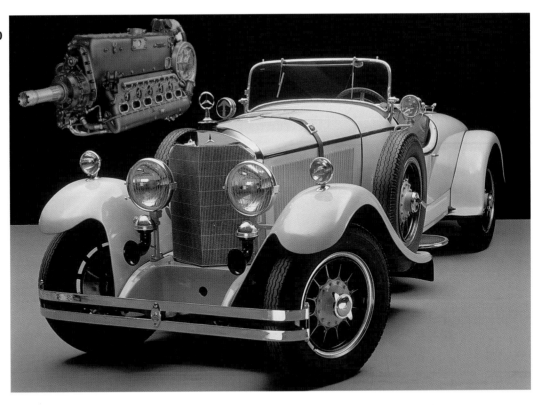

The Mercedes 24/100/140 HP type 630 sport wagon with the (inset) M630 (Monza) engine.

The press release issued on the occasion of the Berlin Motor Show in October 1926 proudly proclaimed:

To satisfy the special needs of the gentleman driver desirous of participating in sporting competitions, Daimler-Benz A.G. has brought out the six-litre Model 'K', which has a peak performance superior to even that of the standard model. It has a top speed of approximately 155km/h (96mph), with special importance having been attached also to maximum reliability of the engine over long distances. The superiority of this vehicle on the international stage is best demonstrated by its numerous successes in speed and reliability competitions as well as by its countless record victories both on the flat and in hill climbs. It is especially noteworthy that, in the Solitude Race of 1926, this standard production tourer was able to defeat the entire field of specialist sports cars and racers on both total time and lap time. The two participating cars crossed the finishing line just seconds apart and in front of all the rest.

Already prior to the Berlin Motor Show, which was the occasion of the above press release, and also in the months

that followed, many independent European motoring magazines expressed extremely enthusiastic opinions on the performance of the top-of-the-line Mercedes model, typically referring to it in terms such as 'Fastest touring car in the world! Superior top speed, maximum reliability. Winner of numerous competitions!'

The Solitude Race, 12 September 1926. Ernst Hailer (start number 26) is at the start with a Mercedes-Benz Model K. He came second and claimed the fastest lap in the class of sports cars over 5 litres.

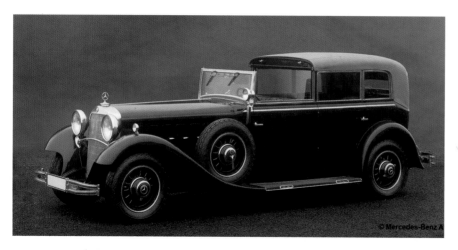

The 5-litre cabriolet version of the Nürburg replaced the coupé tourer of the previous model.

The Grand Mercedes cabriolet was supplied with a hard-top to give it the coupé feel. The last unit of the W07 was produced in October 1938. At the same time, series production of the successor model began, which, unveiled in February 1938, carried the same magical name and was given the in-house design code W150. Official announcements from those years always referred to the W07 as the Mercedes-Benz 'Grand Mercedes' or Model 770 'Grand Mercedes'. The designation 770K, as sometimes found today in the literature, was never used for either the W07 or its successor, the W150.

of the rear wings just above the side running board; these openings affording access to grease nipples for lubricating the spring mountings. On later vehicles, with underslung half-springs, these openings were replaced by a lockable flap that concealed two grease nipples for the front spring shackle.

In February 1928, all Mercedes-Benz passenger cars were given new model designations that were easier to use than the decades-old HP data. In production since 1924, the two 6-cylinder supercharged models, the 15/70/100 HP and the 24/100/140 HP, became the 'Model 400' and the 'Model 630' respectively. The new designations formed the basis of the system that is still more or less in use to this day, in which a three-digit number denotes the displacement in cubic centimetres multiplied by ten.

October 1928 saw changes to the choice of coachwork available for the 400 and 630 models. The five-seater tourer and coupé touring saloon were dropped, as was the removable Pullman top, while a four-/five-seater convertible and a six-/seven-seater Pullman convertible were added to the product range.

There is no simple answer as to what succeeded the 630: candidates include the 'Grand Mercedes', which was unveiled in October 1930, and the 5-litre version of the Nürburg, which was available from February 1931. Both models were less progressive in design than the 24/100/140 HP had been in 1924; nor were they able to cover the entire spectrum of the 630. Although the Nürburg 500 was equally spacious and luxurious, and was also over 30 per cent cheaper, it lacked prestigious appeal as well as the added power of the supercharger. The Grand Mercedes embodied the other extreme: more spacious, more luxurious, and more powerful, it cost over 50 per cent more than the 630.

Through 1926 all members of the model series began to employ the rear-axle suspension used on the K model, with the original cantilever springs being replaced by underslung half-springs. An exterior detail distinguishes the two versions before and after this technical modification: the first version, with cantilever springs, has a small opening in front of each

DMG AND BENZ & CIE MERGER

There had been earlier attempts, during World War I, to unite DMG with Benz & Cie, but it was not till 1924 that they successfully formed a mutually beneficial union. Finally, on 28 June 1926, the two oldest automobile manufacturers in the world merged into one, with the public statement explaining that it was 'in order to be able to offer their customers and commercial vehicles in unbeatable quality at a reasonable price to our global customers'.

The key players in this major merger were the representatives of the banks for each of the companies, Württembergische Vereinsbank for DMG and the Rheinische Creditbank, who were on the board at Benz Cie. It was announced that both banks were to merge with Deutsche Bank, which would in effect make Deutsche Bank a force to reckon with on the board. After DMG's representative at the Württembergische Vereinsbank died suddenly, it made even more sense financially for the two companies to merge in order to safeguard their power, especially as both companies had suffered downturns in assets.

In order to become competitive again, the two southwest German car manufacturers decided to no longer use their energy in the fight against each other, but instead invest it in a 'common cause'.

The two companies had already founded an interest group (IG) in 1924, a form of cooperation that was common at this time, and even though a full merger was considered it was not entered into then for the tax implications.

Strategically, the two companies initially remained differently oriented. DMG wanted to start mass production as quickly as possible and also to install its engines in ships and planes. The integration of a steel mill and a coal mine was also under discussion. However, Benz & Cie wanted to remain with the automotive industry first and foremost, optimizing series production and simplifying the model range to become more competitive before getting deeper into expensive mass production.

The IG agreed to simplify and standardize the product range. In addition, only one vehicle type was to be built in each plant. The 2-litre engines would be manufactured in Mannheim, the 4- to 6-litre engines in Untertürkheim; Gaggenau became the production site for the light trucks under 4 tons, while the heavy trucks were built in Marienfelde. The body shop was concentrated in Sindelfingen.

The name 'Mercedes-Benz AG' was founded as a joint

One of the first advertising posters to celebrate the merger of Benz and Daimler.

sales organization featuring the new Mercedes-Benz brand logo, which was registered as a new trademark in February 1925 and became emblematic of the merger. It combined the Mercedes star from Daimler with the laurel wreath from Benz. The two original trademarks dated from 1909 and, although they had been continuously developed, now became the property of the new company. These early logos and the new Mercedes-Benz brand name appear in many advertisements and other publications by Daimler-Benz AG.

THE 'W' CODE IN BRIEF

The model code scheme dates originally to 1922, before Daimler and Benz merged. The 'W' (for *Wagen*, or car) was

Angemeldet 1909

Angemeldet 1909

Angemeldet 1916

Angemeldet 1926

The amalgation of logos incoporated the three-pointed star of DMG with the wreath of Benz and added the 'Mercedes' name resulting in the medallion number 4.

originally Daimler nomenclature for vehicles and was in turn derived from how the company christened its engines, with an 'M' (*Motor*).

Daimler named an engine for the bore, stroke, and count of its cylinders. For example, its 3.9-litre in-line six was called the M836, a name constructed from the engine's 80mm bore, its 130mm stroke and six cylinders. A digit was plucked from each count, forming Motor 836, or M836. Daimler then gave the car a designation based upon the engine with which it was equipped. An

M836 powered a Wagen 836, which was abbreviated to W836.

After Daimler and Benz combined forces, however, this name scheme became arbitrary. While all new vehicles kept the W prefix, it was now little more than Mercedes' way of chronologically cataloguing its designs. The W01 was the first of these, a series of eight 25hp prototypes that never made production. Its younger sibling, W02, arrived on the market in 1926 as the 8/38 HP, and in doing so, became the first Mercedes with a W model code to roam the roads.

CHAPTER SIX

POST-MERGER MERCEDES AND BENZ

THE 8/38 HP AND STUTTGART 200/260 (W02, W11), 1926–36

Two new models were unveiled in October 1926 at the Berlin Motor Show, the first appearance at a motor show of the newly merged Daimler-Benz AG. Developed by the joint venture, they were the first passenger cars to be marketed under the new brand name of Mercedes-Benz.

In spite of some initial difficulties, the 2-litre passenger car was an instant success, it alone selling over twice as many units in 1927 than the sum of all Mercedes, Benz and Mercedes-Benz models produced in 1926.

The 2-litre 6-cylinder M02 engine had tremendous future development potential. In several stages over a period of twelve years, it provided the basis for higher-displacement engines for subsequent generations of passenger cars: the M11 of 1928 with 2.6 litres, the M18 of 1933 with 2.9 litres and, finally, the M142 of 1937 with 3.2 litres and later 3.4 litres.

As mentioned in the previous chapter, the new W codes

A Stuttgart 200 two-door saloon coupé was added to the range in 1928.

The Pullman landaulet made a return in 1928, albeit in the mid-range Stuttgart 200 series.

introduced with the inception of the Daimler-Benz era were more or less just consecutively allocated design codes devoid of any deeper meaning. Under this classification system, the 8/38 HP was given the in-house code W02, making it the second model to which the new numbering system was applied.

In February 1928, the sales codes of Mercedes-Benz models were also brought up to date: thus the 8/38 HP mutated into the 8/38 HP 200 model and later again, to simplify matters further, it was called the Stuttgart 200. The new model

designation, doubtless more appealing than the rather dry 8/38 HP, related to where the vehicle was produced and was inspired mainly by the name of the new 8-cylinder model that had been launched one month previously as the Nürburg 460.

At the start of sales, the new entry-level model, with the designation 8/38 HP, was available in three different body versions: as an open tourer, a two-door coupé saloon and a four-door saloon. In April 1927, the range was extended to include two two- to three-seater and four- to five-seater

Even as the Stuttgart range was being phased out, a slightly modernized and updated Stuttgart 260 model also included a saloon coupé. The more curving roof line can be clearly seen.

STUTTGART 200 SPECIFICATION

Engine	Front mounted, four in-line M02
Bore × stroke	65 × 100mm
Total displacement	1988cc
Gearing	Three-speed manual
Maximum speed	75km/h (47mph)
Rated output	38bhp at 3,400rpm
Drivetrain	Cardan driveshaft to rear wheels
Wheelbase	2,810mm (111in)
Front/rear track	1,425mm (56in)
Height	1,800mm (71in)
Kerb weight	1,150kg (2,535lb)
Price	RM 8,600

special convertibles. Alternatively, customers also had the option of ordering just the chassis, with coachwork to be added by one of the numerous coachbuilders.

In February 1928, alongside the new designation 8/38 HP 200, some additional measures were taken to promote sales. These involved lowering the sales price and widening the choice of body to a total of eleven variants. The newcomers were a two-seater sports car, a landaulet with open driver's seat and a Pullman landaulet. Then, in July, the range was further extended to include a four- to five-seater short special convertible and a version of the four-door saloon with six windows. The number of available body variants rose to thirteen.

Production of the Stuttgart 260 started in September 1928 and reached volume production level in February 1929, at the same time as manufacture start-up for the standard version of the 2-litre model. Reducing the 2-litre model to the standard version made sense, as the more luxurious and sportier variants undoubtedly benefited from the enhanced power of the 2.6-litre engine. This also found expression in the production statistics: in the year of its launch, the Stuttgart 260 reached a volume of 3,640 vehicles, considerably more than the precisely 2,000 units of its 2-litre counterpart.

Although the life-cycle of the Stuttgart model was nearing its end, stylistically modernized forms of the saloon and convertible were unveiled in October 1932. The saloon now sported a longer engine bonnet, slightly raked windscreen and flowing lines. The Convertible had already been given a raked windscreen one year previously, and now featured a continuous chrome trim strip as well as doors with a lower top edge.

The total production of all 8/38 HP models amounted to 9,105.

MERCEDES-BENZ 5/25 W14 – 'THE CITY COUPÉ'

Derived from the W01 project, the W14 was designed by Ferdinand Porsche in 1928, and gave rise to twenty-eight

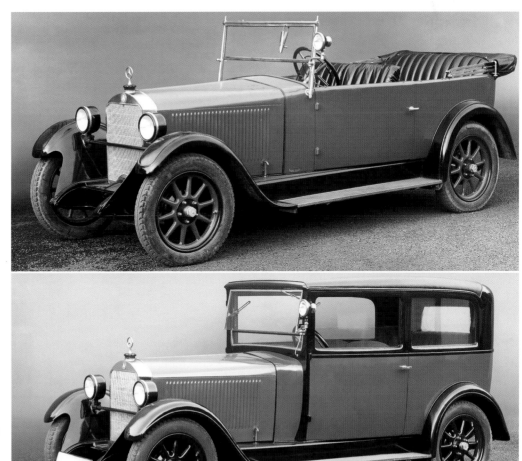

The 1.3-litre-engined W14 never got past its prototype stage but was built as a full saloon, a cabriolet (top) and a coupé saloon (bottom). The public were just not ready for a 'Baby Benz'.

MERCEDES 5/25 W14 SPECIFICATION

Engine	Front mounted, four in-line M14
Bore × stroke	68 × 88mm
Total displacement	1280cc
Gearing	Four-speed manual
Maximum speed	84km/h (52mph)
Rated output	25bhp at 3,300rpm
Drivetrain	Cardan driveshaft to rear wheels
Wheelbase	2,600mm (102in)
Front/rear track	1,340mm (53in)
Height	1,580mm (62in)
Kerb weight	1,000kg (2,205lb)
Price	No production

prototypes. Mechanically, there were many differences. First, the engines no longer had six cylinders but four cylinders in line, with a displacement of 1280cc. The maximum power remained unchanged, but this was reached at 3,300rpm. The four-speed gearbox was also new, resulting in a slightly lower top speed of 84km/h (52mph).

This time around, the managers of the German company were much more convinced and confident of the work of their stellar chief designer, so much so that they were already starting a marketing campaign on the basis of providing an average monthly production of 1,000 specimens. There were also detractors on the board, however, who were not willing to build a 'common city car', so ordered further research. On the back of this, it was decided that the actual earnings compared to the investment required would make building the proposed car decidedly uneconomical, effectively shutting down the W14 project indefinitely.

The twenty-eight prototypes included a cabriolet body, a full saloon and a coupé version.

15/75 HP MANNHEIM 370 S (WS 10), 1931–3

Although this was merely a cabriolet, it marked a point where sporty, coupé-style models were in demand. Customers returned to the sporty saloon for the same reason they opted for a coupé carriage – to show off. Although there were two saloons available (four- or six-seater), the fashionable choice was a four-seat open tourer or convertible.

Only a year after the Nürburg and Stuttgart models, the

The Mannheim crossover from the 15/75 was built as a full four- or six-seater saloon.

The sportier Mannheim 370S cabriolet. The low-slung two-seater bodies were reminiscent of the legendary SSK.

W10 became the third Mercedes-Benz passenger car to be named after a town, and even today, the entire model family from W03 to W10 is collectively referred to as the Mannheim model, even though this designation really applied only to the W10.

Hans Nibel radically slimmed down the vehicle, making the saloon more graceful and lighter. It weighed 200kg (660lb) less and had a 230mm (9in) shorter wheelbase. Because of the extensive modifications, the engine was given the new designation, M10. However, the transmission was now downgraded to a gearshift box with three forward gears instead of the previous four.

The Berlin Motor Show in February 1931 saw two sportily elegant variants to the Mannheim: a convertible with a shorter 3,025mm (119in) wheelbase and a sports convertible with lowered chassis and an even shorter 2,850mm (112in) wheelbase carrying the official model designation 14/75 HP Mannheim 370 K (internal: WK 10, the K standing for 'kurz', or short); and also an even sportier version with still shorter wheelbase called the 14/75 HP Mannheim 370 S (internal: WS 10). This was available as a sports convertible or sports roadster.

770 'GRAND MERCEDES' (W07), 1930–8

The first 'Grand Mercedes' was produced in Stuttgart-Untertürkheim in September 1930 at the end of a two-year development period. When the vehicle was unveiled in October at the Paris Motor Show, it was made clear to everyone that Daimler-Benz was back in business in the high-end segment of international automotive engineering. The Grand Mercedes, or 'Super Mercedes Straight Eight', as it was known in English, was initially available with or without a supercharger. The 7.7-litre 8-cylinder in-line engine had a power output of 150bhp in naturally aspirated mode, with this figure rising to 200bhp when the Roots supercharger cut in at wide-open throttle. In the event, only thirteen out of a total of 117 customers ordered their Grand Mercedes without the supercharger. The Pullman saloon cost a remarkable RM 41,000.

Although there were a number of body versions, including a hard-top version of a cabriolet, there was no official coupé version. As always, though, Mercedes-Benz continued to offer their chassis so that others could fit their own

With the fashion for cabriolet tourers, even the flagship 770 Grand Mercedes was offered as a cabriolet. It went a long way to encourage the design of the coupé.

The 770 was never built as a coupé by Daimler but they always offered chassis versions for customers to design their own. The Neuss Coupé is one such vehicle.

bodies. One such version was built by Neuss in Berlin in around 1930 – and the Mercedes-Benz City Coupé was the result.

THE MERCEDES 200 (W21), 1933–6

Just one and a half years after the launch of the Mercedes-Benz W15 170, whose swing-axle chassis proved both inno-

vative and successful, there followed the next stage in the renewal of the passenger car range. The International Motor and Motorcycle Show in Berlin in February 1933 was the venue for the launch of no fewer than three new models: the 200 (W21), 290 (W18) and 380 (W22).

Initially, the 200 (W21) was nothing more than a slightly more powerful and slightly more spacious version of the W15 170. A 5mm wider bore gave the engine a displacement of 1961cc with a power output of 40bhp, which was 8bhp more than that of the W15 1692cc 170. The wheelbase

The 200 four-seater convertible.

© Mercedes-Benz AG

The 200 two-seater roadster.

© Mercedes-Benz AG

For the first time Daimler added an official two-door saloon coupé to the range in 1934. Later this became the Mannheim Coupé.

on the 200 was 100mm (4in) longer than that of its smaller sibling. The technical concept, in addition to the choice and design of bodies, was the same as for the 170. The 200 replaced the Stuttgart 200, which, with its rigid-axle chassis, was no longer up with the times. Even with its dainty looks, the low-slung swing-axle car lacked the prestigious appearance of its predecessor.

At the beginning, the choice of bodies was still limited. The range consisted of a four-door saloon with an optionally available built-on boot, a convertible and a two-seater special roadster.

With its relatively angular lines and squat, flat radiator, the styling still came across as very stiff, so in an effort to improve sales, the 200 underwent a significant upgrade in time for its second year in February 1934. The squat radiator

made way for the stylistically more pleasing, subtly V-shaped variant more in line with the previous models, which had been the standard face of Mercedes-Benz passenger cars.

The choice of bodies was augmented by two four-seater tourers: a four-door version with a body built in Sindelfingen and, for the first time, a two-door coupé saloon, later called the Mannheim Coupé, albeit for the first five months with third-party coachwork. Both of these versions received a wheelbase of 3,050mm (120in), 350mm (14in) longer than previous models, which improved not only their aesthetic appeal but also their interior comfort. This same wheelbase provided the basis for all the generously sized saloons up until the advent of the 300 in 1951.

In February 1935, a year after the launch of the long-wheelbase version, the sale prices of both chassis types and most body variants were lowered. In addition, the range of bodies was augmented by three new long-wheelbase variants. A four-/five-seater four-door saloon was aimed at addressing many customers' growing need for space. This era also brought with it a new type of customer, one not satisfied with 'just a factory-built automobile', but with an ever-increasing list of demands.

One of these was for a sliding roof; while wishing to drive a saloon, many did not want to forgo the advantages of a roof that could be opened. The standard-wheelbase saloon was optionally available not only with a retractable roof made in Sindelfingen, but alternatively with a sliding roof manufactured by Happich. The long-wheelbase saloon could be ordered at extra cost with a sliding roof from Happich or Webasto, while the Pullman saloon was optionally available with a standard or special-version Webasto sliding roof. In April 1935, the option to order the saloon with a retractable roof made in Sindelfingen was discontinued; instead, as an alternative to the Happich sliding roof, it was possible to order one made by Webasto.

Further modifications for the 1935 model year included larger dials in the instrument panel, a stiffer front end with metal bulkhead against body vibration and a reinforced frame.

The standard-wheelbase two-door coupé saloon was significantly more modern in appearance as well as being more harmonious to the eye than its four-door counterpart, which had been in production for two years; due to the former's popularity, the sales programme was extended by a new version of the convertible based entirely on this two-door coupé saloon.

In view of the spacious though heavy bodies that had been made possible since 1934 by the longer chassis, the 40hp 2-litre engine in the W21 could not really be expected to deliver stunning performance. This called for measures to raise the power output in order to meet growing customer demand.

The solution for the 200 was to increase the engine displacement. The desired increase in displacement to 2.3 litres could not be achieved simply by widening the cylinder bore. Although the bore was widened from 70

© Mercedes-Benz AG

The 200 W21 was given a longer wheelbase in 1935. This is the four-seater cabriolet B.

The long-wheelbase cabriolet A was modelled on the lines of the coupé version.

to 72.5mm, it was additionally necessary to lengthen the stroke by 5mm to 90mm, something that in turn necessitated a new crankshaft. The 2.3-litre engine, with the design code M143, produced 55hp, 15hp more than the M21, and was fitted in the long chassis from May 1936. However, the model designation '200 with long chassis' was initially retained, the 55hp engine being included in the May 1936 price list as an optional extra costing an additional RM 175. Even today, this fact still causes a certain degree of confusion, since although both versions are identical in terms of chassis and body, they carry the

design code W21 or W143, depending on which engine was installed.

Manufacture of the long-version W21 was finally phased out in July 1936, two months after the start of production of the W143. The standard-wheelbase W21 remained in production only in Untertürkheim, where it reached a unit volume of 9,281 vehicles. The long version totalled 6,341 units, with 2,950 being produced in Untertürkheim and 3,391 in Mannheim. It was September 1936 before clarity was restored and the W143 2.3-litre version was given its due designation of '230'.

MERCEDES 200 SPECIFICATION

Engine	Front mounted, six in-line M21	Drivetrain	Cardan driveshaft to rear wheels
Bore × stroke	70 × 85mm	Wheelbase	3,050mm (120in)
Total displacement	1961cc	Front/rear track	1,340/1,380mm (53/54in)
Gearing	Three-speed manual with overdrive	Height	1,600mm (63in)
Maximum speed	93km/h (58mph)	Kerb weight	1,500kg (3,307lb)
Rated output	40hp at 3,200rpm	Price	RM 5,800

HANS NIBEL

Born: 31 August 1880, Olleschau, Moravia
Died: 25 November 1934, Stuttgart, Germany

As chief engineer at Benz & Cie and later Daimler-Benz AG, Hans Nibel played an influential role in developing products at both companies. Among the vehicles he designed were the Lightning Benz (1909), the 770 Grand Mercedes (1930), the Mercedes-Benz 170 (1932) and the W25 Silver Arrow racing car (1934). As a member of the board of management he was also one of the architects of the merger between Benz & Cie and Daimler-Motoren-Gesellschaft (DMG), which led to the creation of Daimler-Benz AG in 1926.

Hans Nibel.

He was born in Olleschau, then part of Austro-Hungary and today in the Czech Republic. As a school report from 1899 illustrates, he was a quick and eager schoolboy, his 'outstanding' grade in subjects such as mathematics, physics and drawing providing an early clue as to the direction Nibel would later follow in his professional life. He enrolled as a student at the Technical University in Munich, graduating with a degree in engineering. He started out in employment with various small engineering works before joining Benz & Cie in Mannheim as an engineer in March 1904 and stayed with the company through its rise to one of the world's leading car makers.

Nibel was soon promoted to deputy office chief, and in 1908 was appointed head of the design department at the age of just twenty-eight. Numerous vehicles were created with his participation and under his leadership, including smaller models that placed the company on a broader commercial footing, such as the 6/14 HP Benz introduced in 1910, but also luxury-class vehicles that acted as global ambassadors for the outstanding automobiles from Mannheim. Another vehicle closely associated with the name Nibel was the Lightning Benz, the fastest and most powerful car in the world at the time. First unveiled in 1909, it established a new world speed record for a car in 1911 of 228.1km/h (141.7mph), a record that would remain unbeaten until 1919.

Such successes quickly advanced Nibel's career. In December 1911, he became an authorized signatory of Benz & Cie. The following year, as if to confirm the achievements of its chief engineer, the company was awarded the Kaiserpreis (Emperor's Prize) for the best German aero engine, another element of the company's product range at the time.

Nibel joined the board of management of Benz & Cie as a deputy member in August 1917. This was not just recognition for his services to automotive design; it also reflected his achievements at Benz & Cie in the years prior to World War I. As was common at the

The Prince Heinrich endurance race (Berlin–Breslau–Tatra–Füred–Budapest–Vienna–Salzburg–Munich) ran 8–10 June 1909. Hans Nibel (start number 703) is at the steering wheel of a 20/35 HP Benz.

time, the production programme had been adapted to meet military requirements, combined with the many new designs that were developed under Nibel's aegis. Throughout, he played a major role in helping to steer the company successfully through these rather difficult times.

Benz & Cie made Nibel a full member of the board of management in August 1922. That same year he was awarded an honorary doctorate by the Technical University, Karlsruhe, in recognition for his services as a designer and engineer. Also in 1922, Nibel worked with Max Wagner, head of the chassis design office in Mannheim, to develop the first streamlined racing cars with individual suspension, an innovation that would soon lead to international racing success. In addition, he was to prove a major influence on the use of diesel engines in road vehicles – in 1922 Benz & Cie introduced an agricultural tractor equipped with a self-ignition engine, the world's first diesel-powered road-going vehicle.

When Benz & Cie and Daimler-Motoren-Gesellschaft formed a community of interests in 1924, Nibel also joined the board of management at DMG. He worked in the same design office and on an equal footing alongside Ferdinand Porsche, although Porsche carried ultimate responsibility.

Nibel was a strong advocate of the merger between the two companies that followed in 1926 – after which he joined the board of management of the new Daimler-Benz AG. That same year, 1926, he switched his workplace once and for all to the Untertürkheim design office of the new company. As an engineer, but also as a member of the company's board of management under the leadership of chairman Wilhelm Kissel, Nibel was a key protagonist in the events that brought about the successful merger between the world's two oldest car makers.

On 1 January 1929, Nibel succeeded Ferdinand Porsche as technical director. He refined his predecessors' vehicle designs, his improvements for example transforming the successes of the 8/38 HP Mercedes-Benz Stuttgart 200 (W02 series), a car that rewarded the brand during the years of the Great Depression with remarkable unit numbers. Nibel also improved the sporty S, SS, SSK and SSKL models (W06, 1926–34) and the elegant Nürburg series (W08, 1929–39), enabling these vehicles to achieve their full impact, whether on the international sporting scene or in the international luxury car market.

The first Grand Mercedes 770 model (W07, 1930–8), which anchored Mercedes-Benz firmly in the collective international consciousness as the brand that built the world's finest cars, was another of Nibel's achievements, for as chief engineer he always answered for and understood the vehicle in its entirety. Among the technical innovations of the Grand Mercedes was a light alloy crankcase with cooling fins and a chromium-nickel steel crankshaft mounted on nine bearings with integrally forged counterweights.

Then came the 170 (W15, 1931–6), which incorporated significant patents, including independent suspension, single-wheel steering and an overdrive gearbox in line with the Mercedes-Benz-Maybach system. The transmission supplied the correct gear ratio for every speed and type of terrain; at the same time, at higher speeds it had the effect of reducing revs and consequently fuel consumption. These and other innovations were also gradually channelled into other model series by Mercedes-Benz. A temporary high point was reached with Nibel's supercharged 380 model (W22), presented in 1932, whose successors were the even more famous 500 K/540 K (W29) models; in particular, these

Presentation of a Nürburg car to Pope Pius XI by Dr Nibel on 23 May 1930.

vehicles raised supercharger technology above the level of sports cars to that of sophisticated luxury automobiles. Their internally produced bodies ('Sindelfingen bodies') set new standards in vehicle design and were acclaimed worldwide.

In 1934, a quite different but no less revolutionary drive concept bearing Nibel's imprint celebrated its world premiere in the 130 model (W23): this vehicle featured a rear engine. Although this car, along with the advance developed (mid-engined) 150 and 170 H models, proved rather unsuccessful as part of the brand portfolio, in technical terms the Nibel design was considered pioneering. Rather more successful was the Mercedes-Benz 170 V (W136, 1936–42), also introduced by Nibel – the first vehicle to feature an X-shaped, lightweight and rigid oval-section tubular frame.

The W25 racing car, designed by Nibel for the 750kg formula, was another vehicle to cause something of a stir. With drivers such as Rudolf Caracciola at the wheel, the car brought the company numerous landmark racing successes between 1934 and 1937 and launched the tradition of the Silver Arrows.

Nibel also left his mark on numerous Daimler Benz aero engines from the 1930s.

On 25 November 1934, Hans Nibel was about to board the express for Berlin at the main railway station in Stuttgart to begin preparations for the 1935 motor racing season when his life was suddenly cut short by a heart attack, robbing the world of one of the most talented engineers of the pre-war era.

The vehicles in which Hans Nibel had a hand influenced the positive image of the Mercedes-Benz brand for many years both before and after his death. Many of his designs remained relevant until well after World War II. As such he can be regarded as one of the most influential automotive engineers, not just of Mercedes-Benz, but of the whole industry. His successor was Max Sailer, who on account of illness was only able to fill the role until the end of 1941. Thereafter Fritz Nallinger took over as chief engineer until his retirement in 1965.

Below is a brief timeline of his career milestones:

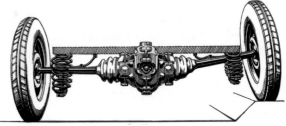

The front wheel twin leaf springs gave an independent element to each wheel, with hydraulic shock absorbers adding to the safety element. The rear wheels of the 170 had independent suspension with swing arm and coil springs.

The W25 racing car was designed by Nibel and incorporated the crossover chassis.

1904 Joined Benz & Cie
1908 Appointed head of the design office
1911 Became head of the design office and authorized signatory
1917 Became deputy member of the board of management
1922 Raised to full member of the board of management. Awarded honorary doctorate by the Technical University, Karlsruhe
1929 Succeeded Ferdinand Porsche as technical director at Daimler-Benz AG
1929 Celebrated twenty-five years of service

SMALL BUT PERFECTLY FORMED

In the late 1920s, ambitious automotive designs were characterized by three things: a move away from the rigid rear axle towards independently suspended wheels; a rear- or mid-engined configuration with a compact drive unit respectively behind or in front of the rear axle; and what was at the time often called a 'Kamm tail' after the Stuttgart aerodynamics expert, but later came to be known as the 'streamlined body'.

The 1921 Rumpler teardrop car with Benz logo, type 10/30 HP, had a 4-cylinder rear engine and rear swing axle.

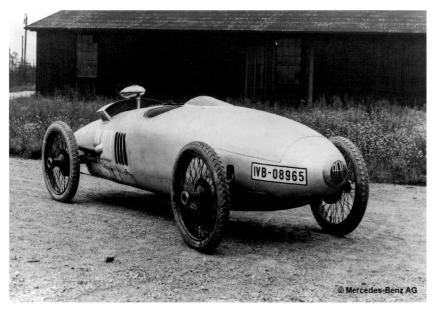

The Benz RH 2.0-litre teardrop-shaped racing car in the Monza racing version from 1923. As can be seen, the driver and co-driver sat very close in the RH cockpit.

The realization that aerodynamics should play a large part in automobile manufacture was set by pioneers such as Edmund Rumpler, Hans Ledwinka, Gustav Röhr and Joseph Ganz, who were also strong advocates of a small, streamlined car. Hans Nibel and Max Wagner also belonged to this group of open-minded engineers willing to abandon old ways in an endeavour to try something new.

Both had worked intensively with innovative design ideas at Benz & Cie in the early 1920s and would later play a leading role at Daimler-Benz in Stuttgart-Untertürkheim in restructuring the passenger car range. At Benz in 1922, they embarked on the development of a state-of-the-art mid-engined racing car. With its avant-garde styling, the vehicle, known only to insiders under its official name of Benz RH ('Rennwagen Heckmotor' or rear-engined racing car), was to make automotive history as the Benz teardrop racing car, named for its distinctive shape. On 9 September 1923, Benz achieved considerable success at the European Grand Prix in Monza, when two teardrop racers finished fourth and fifth despite their inferiority to competitors' cars in terms of power output. What seems a rather modest accomplishment in the usual world of the racetrack was in reality a great triumph. That was also the view of the race organizer, who presented Max Wagner with the prize for the most unconventional racing car in the starting line-up.

The experience gained with the teardrop racing car was to benefit Daimler-Benz in the early 1930s, when challenging economic times called for a broadening of the sales programme to include competitively priced small cars.

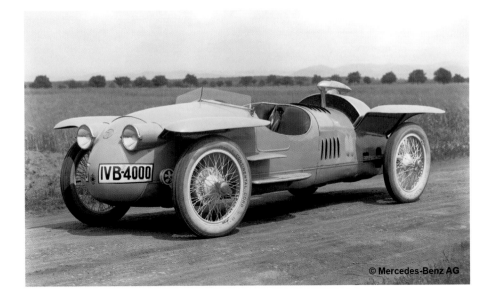

The Benz RH 2-litre teardrop-shaped racing car from 1924, with the three-part front wing arrangement.

© Mercedes-Benz AG

THE REAR-ENGINED COUPÉ

The second half of the 1920s was a period of innovation in automobile technology. Many engineers began freeing themselves from the still-popular designs based on the horse-drawn carriage, with box frame, rigid axles and leaf springs. Instead, they strove towards new solutions such as independent suspension and high-rigidity frames.

The plans of Daimler-Benz AG were influenced by this period of technological progress, for shortly after the merger of Benz & Cie and Daimler-Motoren-Gesellschaft in 1926,

the new company turned once again to the dormant topic of development of the bottom end of the model range. Several designs for smaller vehicles with displacements of 1.3 litres and 1.4 litres were created under Ferdinand Porsche's leadership as chief engineer; some of these were also built for testing purposes. In 1926, these included eight prototypes (W01 series) with a 1.4-litre 6-cylinder engine and an output of 18kW, and in 1928 an additional thirty test vehicles (W14) with a 1.3-litre 4-cylinder engine, which also developed an output of 18kW. However, both cars toed the conventional line with side-valve engines and rigid axle chassis. They

The W01 model prototype of 1926. Based on ideas of Bela Barényi, it went on to be developed into the W23.

never reached the series production stage for economic reasons.

In 1931, Daimler-Benz AG brought to market the Mercedes-Benz 170 (W15), developed by Porsche's successor, Hans Nibel. Although this car proved a great success, there was still a long way to go. Europe did not escape the impact of the global economic crisis during the early 1930s and, realizing the pressing need for an even more affordable vehicle, the company once again opened up a serious internal debate on extending the model range further downwards. Chairman of the board of management Wilhelm Kissel and chief engineer Hans Nibel, in particular, warmed to the challenge of this issue, since before the merger at Benz & Cie the two had enjoyed success with smaller vehicles, including the 8/18 HP Benz of 1911. They were also supported by Max Wagner, head of the design office, and his designer, Josef Müller.

During the late 1920s questions were being raised within the company about the possibility of producing smaller, family-style cars, thinking that perhaps the time for only large, prestigious cars had ended. One thing that everyone agreed upon, however, was that size should never be a reason to sacrifice comfort and ride.

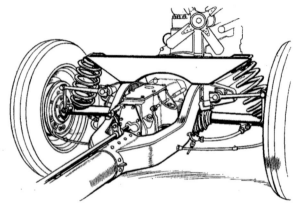

This fundamental principle was clearly revealed in comments made by Dr Kissel:

Although we have to be prudent with our money in these critical years, it is necessary, now more so than ever, to show the world that the spirit of Gottlieb Daimler and Karl Benz lives on in us, and to prove that Daimler-Benz AG is determined to defend its inheritance.

The level of urgency afforded the project was evident from discussions that Kissel had with the board of management and other key figures during the International Automobile and Motorcycle Exhibition (IAMA) in Berlin in 1933. He said:

We are facing the situation in this, the early 1930s, that our position, as well as our plans for a 1.3-litre car, would be considerably enhanced ... if the general outlook does not significantly improve and instead the trend towards smaller, more economical and cheaper cars sooner or later becomes more marked than hitherto. The benchmark remains the position that our sharp focus must be on developing technological progress, because otherwise another company may succeed in producing a car with driving qualities at a price that could thwart our intentions in respect of the 1.3-litre car.

These were certainly difficult times, but Daimler-Benz confronted them head on by going on the offensive. A small Mercedes-Benz with rear-mounted engine was a courageous step forward, and it also injected important new ideas into the automotive world of the 1930s.

The young Josef Müller was one of the avant-garde of automotive engineers striving for fundamentally new technological innovations. In 1932, for example, he pressed ahead with the advance development of a design for cars with a 1.2-litre engine.

Between late 1931 and 1934 the department also came up with numerous designs for small four-seater rear-engined cars with air-cooled boxer engines and liquid-cooled 3- and 4-cylinder engines, some of which were transverse mounted above the rear axle. At the same time, however, vehicles

A number of rear-engined prototypes were built. This one had a rear axle-mounted engine.

were also produced in the same size category with front-mounted engines and front-wheel drive – a pioneering combination at the time. Kissel authorized the front-engine designs to provide a replacement for the rear-engine car if required.

THE W23 130 COMPACT SALOON COUPÉ

Unveiled in 1931, the 170 (W15) boasted so-called swing axles – that is, independently suspended front and rear wheels – but otherwise conformed to the conventional lay-out, with a front engine and rear-wheel drive. The same year saw the launch of the 1.2-litre W17, one of the first Mercedes-Benz rear-engined prototypes. Its air-cooled, horizontally opposed, 4-cylinder ohv engine developed out-put of 25hp, highly impressive by the standards of the day, and many of its key features later contributed to the success of the 'People's Car', the Volkswagen Beetle.

Rare images of the prototype W17.

The production W23 type 130 saloon.

The Nibel and Wagner tubular chassis with independent suspension. The front wheels (inset) were independently suspended with two transverse leaf springs. At the rear, the 130 sported a swing axle with a single coil spring on either side.

While opting for a rear swing axle, the designers decided in favour of a rigid front axle with semi-elliptical springs. The few remaining photos of this prototype show two different body variants: an angular saloon with, in the words of a well-known motoring author, 'all the charm of a coal box', and a streamlined fast-back saloon with thoroughly attractive styling. Neither of the two variants of the W17 went into production, however.

Soon afterwards, the designers in Untertürkheim made another attempt, which this time did make it to the production line. The result was the Mercedes-Benz 130, which was unveiled in March 1934 at the International Motor and Motorcycle Show in Berlin, together with the 500 K autobahn cruiser.

At the time of its launch, the 130, known internally as the W23, was not just Daimler-Benz's smallest series-produced passenger car and the company's first rear-engined model, it was also the world's first mass-produced rear-engined automobile (if one disregards the early vehicles constructed by Karl Benz and Gottlieb Daimler in the nineteenth century).

The Nibel and Wagner-designed 130 sported a tubular backbone chassis that was forked at the rear

Only six units of the type 130 sport saloon coupé were produced.

MERCEDES 130 SPECIFICATION

Engine	Rear mounted, four in-line M23
Bore × stroke	70 × 85mm
Total displacement	1308cc
Gearing	Three-speed manual with overdrive transmission located in front of the rear axle
Maximum speed	92km/h (57mph)
Rated output	26hp at 3,400rpm
Drivetrain	Rear-wheel-drive engine behind the rear axle
Wheelbase	2,500mm (98in)
Front/rear track	1,270mm (50in)
Height	1,510mm (59in)
Kerb weight	980kg (2,161lb)
Price	RM 3,500

to accommodate engine and transmission, the four-speed transmission and the engine being fore and aft of the rear axle respectively. The 4-cylinder water-cooled engine featured standing valves and delivered a power output of 26hp. This engine went on to form the basis for subsequent generations of 4-cylinder in-line units as far as the M136, which was used in the 180 as late as 1957. The front wheels were independently suspended with two transverse leaf springs. At the rear, the 130 sported a swing axle with a single coil spring on either side.

At the time of its launch, the 130 was available as a bare chassis, a two-door coupé saloon, a two-door convertible saloon and two-door tourer.

The rear-engined vehicle's handling soon led to a heated debate. With an axle load distribution of 35 per cent at the front to 65 per cent at the rear, the vehicle proved extremely tail-heavy in on-road use. Hence, as early as 1935, the 130 was relaunched in revised form after a year of development. The improvements related mainly to the body as well as the interior equipment and appointments. Concerns over the vehicle's handling were addressed by changes to the tuning of springs and shock absorbers, modified front wheel camber and less direct steering.

Prominent interior features included two large circular instruments in front of the driver – speedometer and instrument cluster – with their bright dials, in addition to a clock in the glove compartment lid. The rubber mats were replaced by end-to-end carpets, while the front seats now sported superior upholstery and could be adjusted during driving. The footwell was provided with ventilation flaps, which were recognizable from the outside by two slits to the right and left above the front wings. Two-tone paintwork now came as standard, the wings being optionally available in black or in the second vehicle colour.

When this facelift model failed to deliver the hoped-for boost in sales, further attempts were made to address both aesthetic and technical issues; however, neither the 'Autumn Model 1935' nor the 'Winter Model 1935' was able to produce the desired growth in sales for the 130. In February 1936, the unconventional 1.3-litre vehicle gave way to the more powerful and, in many respects, redesigned 170 H. A total of 4,298 vehicles were produced between November 1933 and April 1936.

THE W30 150 SPORT SALOON COUPÉ

In 1934, the 150 (W30) was developed, primarily as a two-seater sport saloon for use in competitions. In its day, it represented a milestone in technological innovation, the importance of which did not become apparent until much later. Based on the 1.3-litre unit from the 130, the engine delivered 55hp, over 100 per cent more than the original product.

MERCEDES 150 SPECIFICATION

Engine	Rear mounted, four in-line M30
Bore × stroke	72 × 92mm
Total displacement	1498cc
Gearing	Three-speed manual with overdrive transmission located in front of the rear axle
Maximum speed	125km/h (78mph)
Rated output	55hp at 4,600rpm
Drivetrain	Rear-wheel-drive engine behind the rear axle
Wheelbase	2,600mm (102in)
Front/rear track	1,300/1,270mm (51/50in)
Height	1,380mm (54in)
Kerb weight	980kg (2,161lb)
Price	RM 6,500

As with its predecessor, the two-door W28 170H came both as a saloon and convertible saloon.

This was made possible, on the one hand, by raising displacement to the 1.5-litre class limit allowed by the sports regulations, and on the other, by replacing the standing valves in the 1.3-litre engine with overhead valves operated by a spur-gear-driven overhead camshaft. The single updraft carburettor gave way to a dual carburettor.

The most significant change compared with the 130 was an improvement to the axle load distribution whereby the engine/transmission drive package was turned through 180 degrees. Engine and transmission were now fore and aft of the rear axle respectively. This mid-engine concept has remained applicable to the present day and is extensively used in motor sport cars and in Formula 1.

The sport saloon, which had just two seats and would

certainly be described as a coupé in modern terms, went on to win four gold medals at the 2,000km endurance race across Germany in July 1934. At the end of the year, the competition vehicle served as the basis for developing the 150 sports roadster (W130), which was exhibited at the International Motor and Motorcycle Show in February 1935, where it caused quite a sensation.

THE W28 170 H SALOON COUPÉ

The W28, 170 H, which superseded the 130, made its debut in February 1936 at the International Motor and Motorcycle Show in Berlin. This was the first and, as far as passenger cars are concerned, the only time that the 'H' for 'Heck-motor' (rear engine) was used officially in the model designation, the identification now being necessary in order to distinguish the rear-engine car from the 170 V, with identical displacement and front-mounted engine. As with its predecessor, the two-door 170 H came both as a saloon and convertible saloon.

The 170 H and 170 V had originally been designed with a 1.6-litre engine. Based on the 1.3-litre engine, this power unit, under development since 1933, had been intended to power the rear-engined model from as early as 1935. The increased displacement, which served above all to generate more torque, was achieved simply by modifying the manufacturing process to increase the bore from 72mm to 73.5mm and by giving the crankshaft a 98mm stroke instead of one of 100mm.

The body of the 170 H, with more harmonious and balanced lines than its predecessor, met with general approval, at least compared to its sister.

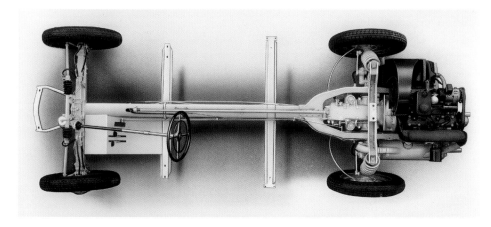

A much-improved backbone chassis provided better stability and comfort.

Its backbone chassis, with its rear fork to accommodate the rear engine, was copied from the 130. The underlying tendency to oversteer that had been present in the 130 was much reduced as a result of careful chassis tuning. Along with improved performance, the rear-mounted engine also significantly reduced engine noise.

Compared with the 130 model, the 170 H had a much more pleasing body form, although in this case the Mercedes star was laid flat on the bonnet and not encircled. The vehicle's appearance remained a hot topic for discussion when it was unveiled to the public at the IAMA. In its reporting on the exhibition, for example, *Motor und Sport* wrote:

The 130 at the rear and the 170 at the front show improvements in style over the production period. DAIMLER CLASSIC CENTRE

Has the general public finally grown accustomed to the shape of the rear-engine car or not? We, at any rate, can find nothing wrong with it. It is a modern car of which one can be proud and one which reveals to the world that its owner is a modern person. We liked the new rear engine automobile with its new four-cylinder 1.7-litre engine very much indeed.

The 170 H differed from the 170 V not just through its avantgarde looks. Although more compact on the outside, the interior of the 170 H was more spacious than the 170 V. In hindsight, without an engine bonnet, the driver's view was similar to that of many more modern vehicles. Stowage space for luggage was improved compared to the 130, although this was not without compromises, since baggage had to be lifted over the back of the rear seats in order to place them in the boot. But this was no different with the equivalent 170 V model; for this class of vehicle, a boot that was accessible from the outside was not introduced until after World War II.

Its compressed-air cooling was an attention-grabber: a blower wheel driven by the alternator shaft forced the air by means of a 'turbo blower' through the coolant radiator, which could be made smaller than usual owing to the forced air supply. The heating system was also a by-product of the compressed-air cooling system, as some of this air passed not only over the enclosed exhaust manifold but also over the silencer. This warmed air was then fed into the vehicle

interior. It was possible both to regulate the heating system and to turn it on and off.

MERCEDES 170 H SPECIFICATION

Engine	Rear mounted, four in-line M28II
Bore × stroke	73.5 × 98mm
Total displacement	1697cc
Gearing	Four-speed manual with overdrive transmission located in front of the rear axle
Maximum speed	110km/h (68mph)
Rated output	38hp at 3,400rpm
Drivetrain	Rear-wheel-drive engine behind the rear axle
Wheelbase	2,600mm (102in)
Front/rear track	1,315/1,270mm (52/50in)
Height	1,600mm (63in)
Kerb weight	1,125kg (2,480lb)
Price	RM 4,350

Like its predecessor, the strictly two-door 170 H was available in saloon coupé and convertible saloon versions. Between July 1935 and October 1939, a total of 1,507 units of the 170 H were built, although success on the sales front was hindered to some extent by the lower-priced, more conservative and, above all, easier-to-drive 170 V.

The reasoning behind this fundamentally 'new concept' for Daimler AG at the time was documented in the original sales brochures of the 1930s:

A rear-mounted engine permitted better use of space. In cars with a relatively short wheelbase, this not only afforded passengers more leg room, it also improved comfort by creating optimum springing between the axles. In addition, the entire drive unit could be focused in a single unit and required no prop shaft, giving vehicles the additional benefit of reduced weight and transmission losses.

It was perhaps to be anticipated that although the concept underwent continual refinements over the years, finally reaching maturity in the shape of the Mercedes-Benz 170 H of 1936, ultimately the rear-engine car never really caught on. When more advanced concepts finally edged forward, many of these special Mercedes-Benz rear-engine vehicles ended up on the scrapheap and very few survived; however, what they did do was to cement the coupé saloon concept in the minds of the consumer public, whether it be a budget family saloon or an executive coupé.

THE 500 K/540 K (W29), 1934–9

For discerning, performance-minded clients, who had been extensively influenced by the large-displacement, high-powered models of the Mercedes-Benz S series, the W22 380, which had been launched just one year earlier, was in many cases seen as underpowered. In March 1934, at the Interna-

The Autobahn Courier 500K in its coupé saloon version.

The 500 K Coupé Streamliner body with rear-set engine was also available from 1934.

tional Motor and Motorcycle Show in Berlin, Daimler-Benz unveiled a new model that was to take over from the W22.

The new 500 'model with supercharger' was exhibited in Berlin in just one version, a so-called 'Autobahn Courier', which, according to the price list for the vehicles on show, 'was specially constructed for particularly high speeds' and was described in a sales department circular as the 'star attraction of the show'.

In June 1934, seven versions of the '500 with supercharger' were added to the price list: there was a four-door saloon, a two-seater roadster with two occasional seats, three convertibles and a two-door open tourer, all at a cost of around RM 22,000. The chassis-only version cost RM 15,500.

The M24 5-litre power plant was based upon the 3.8 M22, although, with the bore and stroke each being increased by 8mm, this also called for a new crankshaft, thus raising the power output to 100/160hp. In official announcements and publications, this 5-litre supercharged model, which was given the internal design code W29, was simply referred to as the '500 supercharged'. Then, at the end of April 1936, the displacement was further increased to 5.4 litres by adding 2mm to the bore, while the stroke was lengthened by 3mm. This increased the power output to 115/180hp.

Even though now more often referred to as the 500 K (for *Kompressor*, meaning supercharger), at the time this nomenclature was not encouraged. This changed, however, with the introduction of the '540 Supercharger': even at its launch, in early October at the Paris Motor Show, it was referred to generally as the 540 K as by now it was thought that sounded a little more memorable.

The 500 K used a Mercedes-Benz overdrive transmission with semi-automatic gearshift. Shifting from third (direct) gear into overdrive did not require use of the clutch. The 540 K initially retained the same transmission albeit now with a direct fourth gear thanks to changed transmission ratios, although in February 1939 it was made available with a five-speed transmission that reduced the revolutions in fifth gear by 20 per cent in comparison with fourth gear.

The chassis of both the 500 K and the 540 K had a wheelbase of 3,290mm (130in) and, as familiar from the 380, was available in two versions. In addition to the standard version, there was a variant in which the radiator, engine/transmission unit, steering gear and seats were all set to the rear by over 100mm (4in). As an additional option not included in the price list, it was also possible to order a chassis with the shorter 2,980mm (117in) wheelbase on which to mount a roadster or convertible body.

Even though the catalogues and price lists from that time give the impression of serial production, these vehicles were extensively custom-built strictly in conformance with the individual wishes and requirements of the customer. With its coachwork for the 8-cylinder sports cars, the special

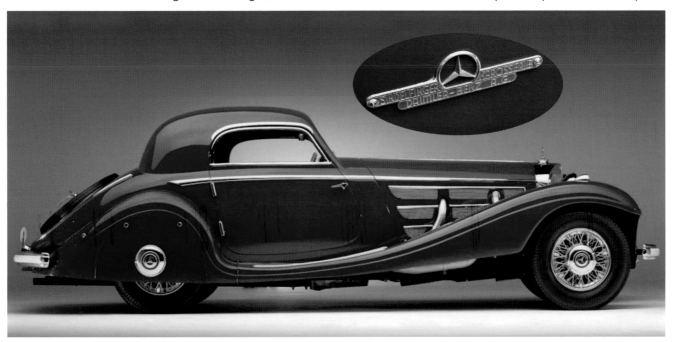

A custom-built 540K was usually known as a 'Sindelfingen Special'. The badge (inset) denoted it was built at home.

A particularly famous example of a custom-built vehicle was the 500 K Coupé of 1935 driven by Rudolf Caracciola (inset), which was known at the time as a 'special coupé' or sport saloon.

vehicle (Sonderwagen) production facility in Sindelfingen under Kurt Ahrens attained a generally acclaimed and virtually unsurpassable standard of beauty and quality of workmanship.

The original range of available bodies for the 500 K was extended in autumn 1934 to include an exceptionally elegant Special Roadster, which was unveiled at the Paris Motor Show in October and which cost RM 4,000 more than the other variants. In February 1935, the four-door saloon gave way to a two-door coupé version. In October 1935, the Paris show witnessed the launch of a new, captivatingly beautiful version of the Special Roadster, which, at RM 28,000, was the most expensive variant of the W29.

From February 1938, the two- and three-seater body versions ceased to be available on the chassis with rear-set engine. The open tourer was also dropped from the February 1939 price list, although interestingly there was an upturn in interest for two body variants that did not show up in any price list: a two-seater sports coupé and the same design in the form of a combination coupé or, to use present-day terminology, a roadster with hard-top.

Irrespective of the variants in the price list or catalogue,

the Sindelfingen factory produced numerous non-standard bodies, sometimes in response to specific customer requests and sometimes on their own initiative. With the 180hp developed from the supercharged 540 K 8-cylinder engine, it was obvious the car was something of a performer and, although the long, wedged-shaped nose, sweeping tail and elegantly contoured wings gave the car an ample touch of luxury, the emphasis on performance also gave the body styles quite an aggressive look. Most customers ended up swinging a little more towards the side of sports car performance style, and Sindelfingen would end up producing far more cabriolets than coupés – only about seven 540 Ks were produced with coupé bodies.

In 1934, Wilhelm Haspel recommended to Silver Arrows team driver Rudi Caracciola the Autobahn Courier 500 K Coupé as an eminently practical automobile for a driver who needed to criss-cross Europe in all weather conditions to race the W25 model GP car. It was a fastback five-window design with teardrop wings.

Two were built in total on each of the 500 K and 540 K chassis. Hermann Ahrens' Sonderwagen facility completed the first Autobahn Courier in only ten weeks in order to make its auto show debut, proving the shop's ability to create a completely new and dramatically different design on an abbreviated schedule.

Between February 1934 and November 1939, the Unter-türkheim plant produced a total of 761 chassis of the two W29 models, 342 with 5-litre displacement and 419 with 5.4-litre versions. Seventy chassis were supplied to specialist coach-builders, while the other 691 units were fitted with bodies at the special vehicle production facility in Sindelfingen.

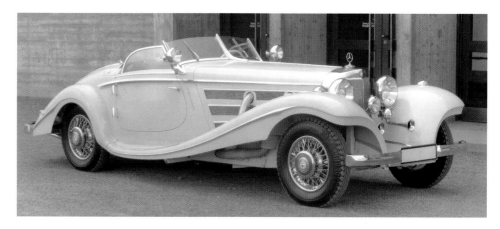

The Special Roadster defined the Art Deco period of automotive design.

The top seller was the convertible B with 296 units, followed by the convertible C and convertible A with 122 and 116 vehicles respectively. Even the exclusive Special Roadster had a total production run of around fifty units, whereas only twelve of the various coupé variants were manufactured, with as few as six buyers being found for the Autobahn Courier. The statistics were rounded off by fifty-three saloons and twenty-eight open tourers.

Enthusiast magazines of the time were unremitting in their praise. One described the 500 K with these words: 'This is a master car for the very few. The sheer insolence of its great power affords an experience on its own. The design and construction throughout are typically thorough and well-executed.'

Of the 540 K, another said: 'As a piece of engineering, it stands unsurpassed. It is amongst the most luxurious, as well as the fastest, touring cars in the world.'

SINDELFINGEN

Daimler-Benz concentrated automobile coachwork production at Sindelfingen, a massive facility that had developed a combination of medium-volume production methods for high-quality coachwork and a select group of designers and craftsmen who conceived, created and built low-volume, nearly custom, bodies for the finest chassis in the Mercedes-Benz line and crafted a few highly specialized bodies for the most demanding clients.

Although Sindelfingen had been constructed during World War I to build aircraft, the Treaty of Versailles that ended the war prohibited aircraft construction in Germany on the industrial scale, so Hans Klemm, the factory's manager, eventually reorganized the factory to build automobile, truck and bus bodies. Sindelfingen was alive once again and continued to employ classic coachwork construction techniques with wood frameworks and sheet metal panels throughout its early history; following the 1926 merger of Mercedes-Benz, it also added high-capacity steel presses of 750 and even 1,000 tonnes to stamp out large, complex panels, particularly wings.

Sindelfingen's aircraft-building history manifested itself in a facility-wide devotion to quality that remained central to its operation throughout the 1930s. Specialized tools, fixtures and machines were designed and built in its own shops. Processes were meticulously planned and documented. A strict quality-control system inspected every single body, whether it was for a modest 170 H or an elegant Grand Mercedes 770 Pullman limousine.

Klemm was succeeded by Josef Bildstein, who later took over Daimler-Benz's Mannheim factory and turned over management of Sindelfingen to Wilhelm Haspel, under whose leadership the factory became a major success for Daimler-Benz. It was a complicated undertaking in which every aspect of coachbuilding was integrated, from selecting and drying the beech and ash used for framing through stamping and forming metal panels to final assembly and painting.

Every kind of bodywork, from one-off and low production bodies for the 500 K, 540 K and Grand Mercedes to volume production of Mannheim's 170 H and V, truck cabs, specialized truck bodies, buses and even contract work in

Strict quality control of the line meant reliability and efficiency for every model of Mercedes, from the smallest to the biggest.

volume for BMW and Wanderer was undertaken at Sindelfingen. Haspel's success at co-ordinating this diverse facility was rewarded with his later promotion to Daimler-Benz managing director in 1942.

In September 1932, Hermann Ahrens joined Mercedes-Benz from Horch to head the Sonderwagen (special vehicles) section, designing and building limited production coachwork for the top Mercedes-Benz models. Ahrens would design and oversee construction of all limited-production Mercedes-Benz coachwork for nearly forty years, including the great sports roadsters and coupés on the 8-cylinder supercharged chassis. It was his artistry that created the magnificent sweeping, partially skirted wings, integrated running boards and deftly shaped passenger compartments and doors that so effectively complemented the imposing

long hoods and exterior exhaust pipes of the supercharged 500 K and 540 K.

Mercedes-Benz produced almost all the coachwork for even the most expensive and luxurious of its automobiles. According to the research of Jan Melin, just eighty-nine of the 928 chassis built for the 380, 500 K and 540 K were supplied to outside coachbuilders. That is a mere 9.6 per cent, a tiny portion of the total production and largely unprecedented among luxury automobile manufacturers in the 1930s.

The combination of superb engineering, high-quality materials, meticulous quality control and inspired design of the supercharged 8-cylinder Mercedes-Benzes with the limited-production coachwork of Sindelfingen brought into existence some of the finest and most respected automobiles of all time.

The Sindelfingen Karosserie (bodywork) department could take care of every customer need.

THE 320 (W142 IV), 320 N COMBI COUPÉ AND COUPÉ

In February 1937, the International Motor and Motorcycle Show witnessed the launch of the 320, the successor to the 290. At the Berlin show, predecessor and successor stood side by side in harmony. The 290 was still in production, at least in the long version, and was still included in the price list. It was only in May, one month after production of the 320 had started, that the 290 long was finally phased out.

Its successor was given an enthusiastic reception by customers, mainly on account of its higher power output – even over sixty years ago, the 290's 68hp was not found to be wildly excessive. The 320's extra 10hp and 10 per cent greater displacement rebalanced the relationship between power and weight, something that had been lacking in the otherwise extremely harmonious predecessor model.

The chassis and suspension were broadly the same as in the 290. Consequently, the 320, too, was available in a choice of two different wheelbases. Just as with the 200 and 230 mid-size models, Mercedes-Benz's luxury-class offering also experienced a discernible shift of customer interest from short- to long-wheelbase variants. This trend was reflected in how the two variants were named. As already with the 230, the long version of the 320 was given the simple model designation without an additional letter, while the shorter-wheelbase variants of both models were distinguished by an appended 'N' (in upper or lower case).

The main externally visible differences between the 320 and the broadly similar 290 were the slightly less weighty bumpers, which now sported horns, and the modified look of the radiator. Somewhat smaller in diameter, the head-lamps were enclosed inside more spherical housings, which were attached directly to the wing on cast legs. This dispensed with the need for the striking, chrome-plated transverse rod in front of the radiator.

The range of bodies for the 320 N was significantly reduced in comparison with the predecessor model: apart from the chassis-only version, the choice now included just a two-/three-seater convertible A and, for the first time, a two-/three-seater 'combination coupé'.

With the ever-changing evolution of fashionably styled automobiles, the Combi Coupé was offered as a multi-use automobile, a high class limousine, a coupé-bodied grand tourer with its hard-top attached and a convertible roadster with it removed.

Despite the highly pleasing lines of its bodies, the 320 N (long wheelbase) apparently failed to live up to expectations and was no longer included in the price list of February 1939.

In early 1939, the variants with the 3,300mm (130in)

The 320N 'Combination Coupé' offered drivers full open-air motoring with close to coupé feel.

The 320 chassis-only version was used by Sindelfingen to produce two true coupé models later referred to as the Reise Coupé (travel coupé), one for Rudolf Caracciola and the other for Manfred von Brauchitsch.

Despite growing competition between 1937 and 1940, the 320 was able to maintain its position in the market segment for large comfortable touring cars. It was only the war that prevented further sales successes and higher production volumes. The 320 was produced at the Daimler-Benz parent plants in Mannheim and Untertürkheim. The last 320 vehicles rolled off the assembly line in Mannheim in September 1939, while production in Untertürkheim continued until November 1942. A total of 6,861 vehicles were built, 1,764 of them being in the form of the Kübelwagen utility car for the Wehrmacht.

wheelbase underwent modification. The engine displacement was increased to 3405cc by adding 2.5mm to the bore, mainly to avoid having to reduce the power output in view of a deterioration in petrol quality. Notwithstanding these changes, the model designation 320, as well as the design codes W142 and M142, were retained. In view of the growing use of autobahns, the 320 was provided with an additional ZF cruising gear as standard. This consisted of a planetary gear behind the normal four-speed transmission, which reduced the engine speed by 25 per cent. This autobahn cruising gear was engaged using a separate lever. At the same time, a coolant remote thermometer was added to the standard equipment package.

There were also innovations on the body front: the saloon with streamlined body was dropped, and the Pullman saloon was provided with a so-called 'add-on boot' instead of the integrated luggage rack. The add-on boot was a permanently mounted luggage compartment organically joined to the rear wall of the body.

MERCEDES 320 SPECIFICATION

Engine	Rear mounted, four in-line M142-1
Bore × stroke	82.5 × 100mm
Total displacement	3208cc
Gearing	Four-speed manual with overdrive transmission located in front of the rear axle
Maximum speed	130km/h (81mph)
Rated output	78hp at 4,000rpm
Drivetrain	Rear-wheel-drive engine behind the rear axle
Wheelbase	2,880mm (113in)
Front/rear track	1,475/1,500mm (58/59in)
Height	1,500mm (59in)
Kerb weight	1,725kg (3,803lb)
Price	RM 12,300

CHAPTER SEVEN

POST-WAR MERCEDES-BENZ

DIFFERENT ROUTES FOR THE USA AND EUROPE

Although in the aftermath of World War II times were hard in Europe, as economic conditions begun to improve slowly this had a great effect on the motor market. To a large extent, automotive design in Europe and the USA went down different routes. Europe had been economically brought to its knees by the war and its mobility needs and, even though cars were mostly still shaped and constructed by hand, focus remained on cheaper small cars, and appearance, at least for the time being, was of secondary importance.

In the USA, on the other hand, the car was a status symbol, and Americans revelled in excessive dream car designs. Customers lusted after panoramic windscreens, fintails and aggressive radiator grilles. Individual components, such as bumper horns, wing tips and even wheel trims, were accorded special styling and emphasis, usually involving lots of chrome plating.

New design principles in car building meant that the days of independent bodybuilders were fast coming to an end. One reason for this was the introduction of the self-supporting body, a design approach that no longer required a chassis in the traditional sense of the term. Those parts that would previously have been mounted on the frame were now attached to the body directly.

At Mercedes-Benz, too, a new era was underway. Although various successor versions of the W136 170 model were built until 1955, abandonment of pre-war design had begun as early as 1951, if only cautiously to begin with. It was the

© Mercedes-Benz AG

The new W187 220, looking more modern than its predecessor, the W136 170.

W187 220 model that set things rolling. Basically, this was a 6-cylinder version of the 170 S, although the designers had restyled its front wings and integrated the headlamps into the wings, where they had hitherto been squashed between wings and radiator grille. Now, with headlamps mounted further apart, the 220 suddenly had a much more modern countenance.

THE 300 AND START OF THE PONTON ERA

The same year also saw the advent of the Mercedes 300 model W186, colloquially known as the '300er' or simply the 'Adenauer', since this was the vehicle of choice of the first chancellor of the new Federal Republic of Germany. The 'Adenauer' clearly demonstrated the transition from the classic shape with freestanding wings and headlamps to the self-supporting chassis-body structure ('Ponton' design). Set wide apart, the headlamps were integrated into the wings, whose momentum continued deep into the front doors. The rounded wings also helped to compensate visually for the rather bulky front end and oversized volumes.

Another member of the 300 family was the W128 300 S Coupé. Based on the shortened 300 chassis, this car continued the tradition of the large saloon coupé. Its front and rear wings retained an individual profile – one of the last

cars to do so. As such, therefore, the 300 was considered an elegant farewell to traditional automotive design. Werner Breitschwerdt, who later took over as head of body development at Sindelfingen and would eventually become chairman of the board of management of Mercedes-Benz, said of this coupé: 'It was by some distance the most beautiful car of its era.'

For the Mercedes automobile, the future belonged to the self-supporting body. In the USA, the Ponton era had come in as early as 1946, whereas the first European vehicles to feature this smooth-surfaced, simplified body form stripped of running boards, protruding wings and separately mounted headlamps were not seen until 1950. The days of frame construction were numbered; from now on all modern automobiles would feature self-supporting bodies.

Mercedes-Benz surprised the automotive world in 1953 with the all new W120 180 model, the first Mercedes-Benz vehicle to adopt this new style. Mercedes had now completely integrated the wings into the basic body, while also featuring continuous side flanks that continued from front engine compartment to a 'booted' luggage compartment in the rear. Out of this design also arose a harmonious and, by modern standards, generously proportioned glazed passenger compartment; it soon became known as the 'three-box design'.

With this three-box design, or Ponton, as the vehicle became known colloquially, Mercedes said farewell to the

Mercedes 300 model W186, colloquially known as the '300er', or simply the 'Adenauer'.

The W180 three-box design revolutionized build strength and safety.

German aesthetic ideal of pre-war cars. The rectangular outline of the new 180 offered distinct advantages: a more spacious interior and vastly improved aerodynamics combined with much reduced wind noise, thanks to the sleek, solid front end. Compared to that of the previous 170, the interior had grown by 22 per cent, the luggage compartment by an astonishing 75 per cent and the window area of the body by 40 per cent.

The stylistic break of the first Ponton Mercedes from its predecessors was a major risk nonetheless. To soften the change, Daimler-Benz sought to introduce such innovation in parallel with a number of evolved design elements that were in keeping with the design tradition; for example, the 180 continued to feature a noticeably lower bonnet, culminating in the typical Mercedes radiator grille, albeit canted slightly into the oncoming

The self-supporting body, which in the 180 was also bolstered by a frame-floor assembly, made the vehicle lighter and more torsionally rigid than its predecessor models, improving both agility and handling. It was these features that would attract customers' attention.

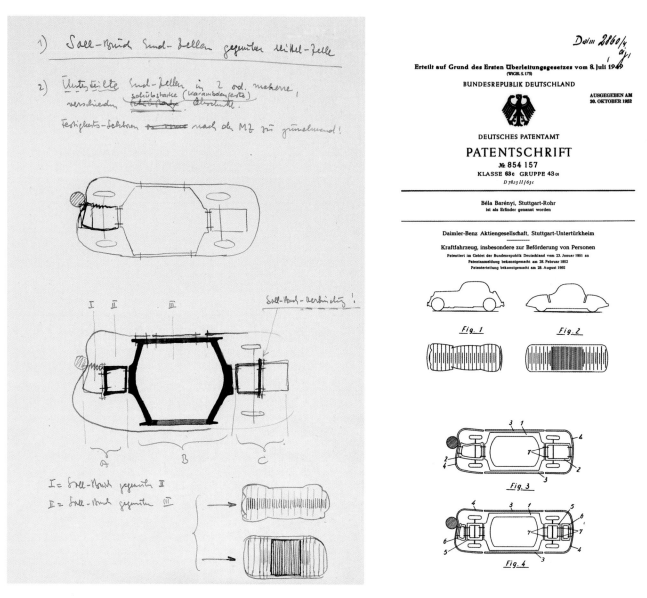

Rough sketch by Béla Barényi for his crumple zone concept, here called 'end cell with predetermined break point', alongside the 1949 patent.

wind. The circular headlamps were set into the dynamically sculpted front wings. The elegant rear end fell away gently towards the tail, giving a perception of momentum, reminiscent of the dynamic lines of pre-war automobiles; this same, typical Mercedes design element reappears often through the years right into the modern day.

Auto-Kraftrad wrote: 'It was a very clever idea not to "lose face", despite adaptation to the international standard and the resulting change of shape, and to allow the world-famous emblem, the attractive three-pointed star, to accentuate the vehicles' exclusivity.'

DESIGNED IN SAFETY

The advancements in body structure and the move away from the solid ladder structure of the separate chassis brought with it many opportunities to improve safety; how-

BÉLA BARÉNYI

Born: 1 March 1907, Hirtenberg, Vienna, Austria
Died: 30 May 1997, Stuttgart, Germany

Barényi was born into one of the wealthiest Austrian families in Austria-Hungary and so from an early age he was able to enjoy riding in a car: his family owned an Austro-Daimler, which he grew to love as a small boy. When World War I broke out, little Béla's fortunes changed, however. When he was only ten years old, his father was killed in action.

Béla Barényi.

Little by little, the war and the ensuing Great Depression swallowed up all the family's wealth. The financial disaster was so great that he even had to stop attending school for a time because his widowed mother could no longer afford to pay his school fees.

Béla found ways and means to enrol as an engineering student at the Viennese Technical College of Mechanical and Electrical Engineering in 1924. The young student's feel for future trends was astonishing: one of his first design projects was the front end of an automobile where the end piece of the body was a horizontal piece, bordered by two horizontal body ends. The horizontal piece as a predominant stylistic element was to be called the 'New Look' a few years later – and to be integrated into many automobiles.

In 1926, Barényi graduated from the technical college in Vienna with excellent marks. This was also the year that Daimler-Motoren-Gesellschaft (Daimler Motor Company, DMG) merged with Benz & Cie. The Great Depression followed a few years later. Bans on recruitment, bankruptcies and large-scale redundancies became the rule of the day, even for such a gifted designer. Up until the mid-1930s, he had to survive on temporary posts as a draughtsman and from freelance work as the author of technical treatises. The fact that his ideas were often ahead of their time did not save him from being the victim of redundancy himself.

It was not until almost a decade after graduating that he was offered his first steady job at the Gesellschaft für technischen Fortschritt (GETEFO, the Society for Technical Progress) in Berlin, later moving to its French partner company, SOPROTEC, in Paris. It was there that he met his future wife, Maria Kilian.

In his student days Barényi already thought about the 'future people's car'. Sketches he made in 1924–5 prove that he was the intellectual father of the 'people's car' or 'Volkswagen'.

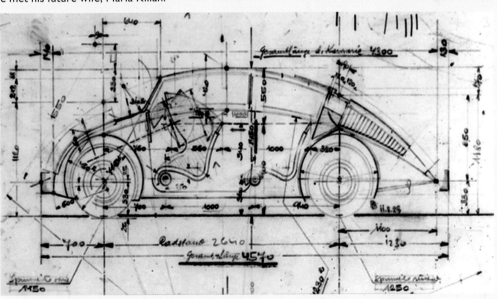

The first Mercedes-Benz vehicle with bodywork developed according to this patent was the 1959 W111 series, colloquially known as the 'Tailfin'. All in all, this discovery was to revolutionize the entire automotive industry.

In the time when he worked for GETEFO/SOPROTEC alone, he registered over 150 patents. But his days at GETEFO were numbered: at the beginning of 1939, he was once more out of a job. Desolated, he searched for a new position. That was when he recalled his childhood dream: the Austro-Daimler. He applied to Mercedes-Benz and was turned down. Feeling he had nothing to lose, he tried his luck again. This time he was given the opportunity to prove his abilities to chairman Wilhelm Haspel in a one-to-one interview. Béla Barényi presented himself as the passionate perfectionist he was. He did not mince words, telling Haspel directly everything that was being done wrong in the design department. Haspel recognized the young man's enormous potential: 'Mr Barényi, you are fifteen to twenty years ahead of your time. You will be put under a bell jar in Sindelfingen. Everything you invent will go straight to the patent department.' Barényi never had to write a job application again.

The thing that Mercedes-Benz and the designer had in common was their passion for safety. This was back in the days when car manufacturers carefully avoided using the term; particularly in the post-war period, nobody wanted to be reminded about the dangers of driving. The topic was viewed as a sales killer right up to the 1970s. Béla Barényi, however, did not let this put him off.

His biggest breakthrough came in 1951 when he registered patent DBP 854.157, commonly known as the 'crumple zone'. Béla Barényi was the first to recognize – years before, in fact – that kinetic energy should be dissipated by deformation to avoid harming the occupants of the vehicle.

Barényi was an inventor through and through. The expression 'time to go home' only meant one thing for him: that he had to change locations to carry on experimenting. Numerous patents and designs, from the Ponton body to the pagoda roof, from the 'disappearing windscreen wiper' to the deformable steering column, can all be attributed to him.

In 1966, Barényi, together with Mercedes-Benz's member of the board of management for development, Hans Scherenberg, defined the division of safety into active and passive safety. This separation still applies to the entire automotive industry to this day. In concrete terms, active safety concerns driving aspects and passive safety deals with protection measures for vehicle occupants and pedestrians.

Another innovation that Barényi endorsed saw Mercedes-Benz engineers employ data taken from actual traffic accidents that involved their cars. From 1969, his department both analysed and carried out reconstructions of real-world crashes. In addition, he instituted a programme of experimental safety vehicles, which began in the early 1970s, as part of a world-wide research programme. Of more than thirty ESVs designed by Mercedes-Benz to research future automotive safety systems, the company presented four vehicles based on the 114 and 116 model series to the public, culminating in 1974 in a version of the W116 S-Class that debuted driver airbags, anti-lock brakes and belt tensioners, all of which were features of the production W126 series of 1979.

In 1972, Barényi retired but he was never forgotten: the Deutsches Museum in Munich organized a Béla Barényi exhibition and in Europe two roads were named after him. He became honorary member of the Deutsche Aktionsgemeinschaft Bildung-Erfindungen-Innovationen (the German Action Group for Education, Inventions and Innovations), was awarded a professorship by the federal president of Austria, and was endowed with the Cultural Award for outstanding achievement in the field of science by the city of Baden – to name but a few of the honours that were bestowed on him. In the 1990s, when the subject of safety became a central theme in advertising, there could be only one possible protagonist for the Mercedes-Benz commercials: Béla Barényi.

Today people are honoured in his name for outstanding achievements in the field of traffic and automotive transport: the Béla Barényi Prize has been awarded in Vienna since 2005.

The conical door lock pin to stop doors opening after impact.

The steering column and wheel would deform when the vehicle was hit to protect the driver from chest injuries.

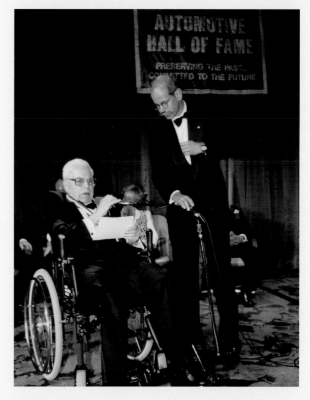

In 1994, Barényi was received into the Automotive Hall of Fame in Detroit and welcomed into the circle of outstanding inventors and innovators.

Body model 220SEb from the W111 series; the curved longitudinal members permitted controlled deformation of the crumple zones.

ever, not everyone was convinced, sceptics claiming that 'a car is only safe if it is solid'.

Enter Béla Barényi, who discovered this was a misconception because it meant that the impact energy was passed on to the occupants with fatal consequences. By 1950, Barényi concluded that the safest structure was deformable parts in the body along with a stable passenger cell in the middle, which would dissipate the energy enough to lessen the consequences on a human body in the event of a collision.

On 28 August 28 1952, the crumple zone idea with the three cells was patented.

According to the original description, the main claim of this patent is 'that the chassis and body are dimensioned in such a way that their strength is greatest in the area of the passenger compartment and decreases gradually towards the extremities of the body'.

The construction revolutionized car manufacturing because the patent was copied by the competition. In view of the patent infringements, however, Daimler-Benz was surprisingly far-sighted and did not take any legal action against it. The reason for this charitable response was that 'safe cars from all manufacturers were considered the higher good'.

The result was that the former taboo topic of automobile safety slowly became a selling point.

THE 220 (W187) 1953–5

At the first Frankfurt International Motor Show in April 1951, Daimler Benz unveiled the W187 range of passenger car – models 220 and 300. Both had a brand-new ohc 6-cylinder engine. Except for its 2.2-litre engine with 80bhp, the 220 model was based mainly on the 170 S.

The chassis and car bodies were almost identical, with the headlights integrated into the front wings, which had

been modified accordingly. In order to do justice to the significantly higher engine power, the front wheels of the 220 model were equipped with duplex brakes.

Like the 170 S, the 220, which first went into serial production in July 1951, was offered with three different car bodies, the saloon, Convertible A and Convertible B, the latter two being positioned as exclusive and sporty GT cars. They replaced the corresponding versions of the 170 S, production of which ended in November 1951.

Apart from the body types already mentioned, the 220 model was also available as a chassis for special bodies. In October 1952, eight ambulance cars were produced at Lueg in Bochum and, between October 1952 and July 1954, more than thirty police radio cars were built by the bodybuilder Binz in Lorch on the basis of the 220 chassis.

In November 1953, the straight front window of the Convertible A was replaced by a slightly curved one to underscore the sporty appearance of this model. From December 1953, 'after repeated requests of some important persons' as it was put in a circular letter of the sales manager, another body type was produced: a coupé, which, because of its high price and small manufacturing scale, became the most exclusive version of the 220 model. Technically as well as stylistically, the Coupé was based on the Convertible A.

In terms of sales price and the number of units produced, the Coupé became the most exclusive version of the W187 series – just eighty-five units of this model were manufactured, whereas the combined production volume of all the other versions came to more than 18,400, including 1,278 Convertible A units. Exclusivity was also expressed by the price: the Coupé cost 20,850 Deutschmarks – DM 22,000 with steel sunroof (December 1953) – while the Convertible A cost DM 18,850 (February 1952); by comparison, the saloon, with a price tag of DM 11,750 (February 1952) looked decidedly inexpensive.

The W187 220 Coupé was based on the Convertible A/B.

The exclusivity of the coupé came at double the price of the saloon version.

MERCEDES 220 (W187) SPECIFICATION

Engine	Front mounted, four in-line M180-1
Bore × stroke	80 × 72.8mm
Total displacement	2195cc
Gearing	Four-speed manual
Maximum speed	150km/h (93mph)
Rated output	80bhp at 4,000rpm
Drivetrain	Rear-wheel drive via Cardan shafts
Wheelbase	2,845mm (112in)
Front/rear track	1,315/1,435mm (52/56in)
Height	1,550mm (61in)
Kerb weight	1,720kg (3,792lb)
Price	DM 20,850 (DM 22,000 with sunroof)

From April 1954, the Coupé and Convertible A were equipped with an engine with a higher compression ratio and a higher output of 63kW, a unit which had already been developed for the successor model, the 220a, production of which began in June 1954.

Production of the 220 saloon was discontinued in May 1954, the last Convertible B having come off the assembly line in Sindelfingen one year earlier. The Coupé and Convertible A continued to be built until July and August 1955 respectively. More than a year was to pass before three-box body versions of the coupé and cabriolet became available from the new Mercedes-Benz 220 series.

THE 300 S AND 300 SC COUPÉS (W188), 1951–8

The W188 marked an exclusive start to a new coupé tradition, a return to what the coupé always was – an individual, high-class saloon in a sporting two-door body.

In October 1951, Daimler-Benz launched the Mercedes-Benz 300 S at the Paris Motor Show one month before production of the 300 saloon (W186) began, giving Daimler two top-of-the-range models in its portfolio. The 300 S was positioned as a representative car with a sporty touch, meeting the highest demands on road-holding, safety and speed. Its success was reflected in the verdicts of the international motoring press, which described the new model as

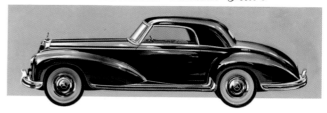

MERCEDES-BENZ »Type 300 S« SPORT COUPÉ

MERCEDES-BENZ »Type 300 S« SPORT ROADSTER

MERCEDES-BENZ »Type 300 S« SPORT CABRIOLET

Promotional advert for the 'stars of the show'.

'the car for the world's elite' and 'the yardstick for what is feasible in contemporary automotive engineering'.

In technical terms, the 300 S was largely based on the saloon version of the 300 model (W186) but had a 140mm (6in) shorter chassis. Engine output was boosted to 110kW through an increase in the compression ratio and the fitting of as many as three carburettors, giving the car a top speed of 175km/h (109mph). Alongside the Coupé, the 300 S was also offered in Cabriolet A and roadster versions. Production of the three variants started between June and September 1952; of the Coupé, a total of 216 examples were built during the following four years.

At the Frankfurt International Motor Show in September 1955, Daimler-Benz presented a revised saloon, the Mercedes-Benz 300c, and an equally refined version of the 300 S. The most important modifications had been made

The critically acclaimed 300 S Coupé remains an exclusive model to this day.

The 300 Sc Coupé had various embellishments and a fuel-injected engine.

MERCEDES 300 SC COUPÉ SPECIFICATION

Engine	Front mounted, six in-line M199
Bore × stroke	85 × 88mm
Total displacement	2996cc
Gearing	Four-speed manual
Maximum speed	180km/h (112mph)
Rated output	175bhp at 5,400rpm
Drivetrain	Rear-wheel drive via Cardan shafts
Wheelbase	2,900mm (114in)
Front/rear track	1,480/1,525mm (58/60in)
Height	1,510mm (59in)
Kerb weight	2,000kg (4,409lb)
Price	DM 36,500

MERCEDES 300 S COUPÉ SPECIFICATION

Engine	Front-mounted, six in-line M188
Bore × stroke	85 × 88mm
Total displacement	2996cc
Gearing	Four-speed manual
Maximum speed	175km/h (93mph)
Rated output	150bhp at 5,000rpm
Drivetrain	Rear-wheel drive via Cardan shafts
Wheelbase	2,900mm (114in)
Front/rear track	1,480/1,525 mm (58/60in)
Height	1,510mm (59in)
Kerb weight	2,000kg (4,409lb)
Price	DM 34,500

on the rear axle and the engine. Like the saloon, the refined coupé, internally named 300 Sc, now had a single-joint swing axle with a low pivot point. Fuel mixture was no longer by three carburettors but by direct injection; with the compression ratio raised at the same time, this boosted engine output to 129kW. The original brochure had this to say:

The felicitous combination of the highest performance and driving safety with refined elegance and unique quality has caused the Mercedes-Benz 300 S to quickly become a car of choice in the international luxury class. It is the world's first large touring car to feature a direct-injection engine modelled on the famous 300 SL production sports car.

The bodywork had also been modified in several respects. The 300 Sc had quarterlights next to the side windows as well as larger direction indicators at the front and rear. Other distinguishing features were two horizontal, chrome-trimmed ventilation louvres on both sides underneath the engine hood, as well as chrome strips running all the way from the front to the rear wheel cut-outs. Reference to the more powerful engine was made in the form of the chromed lettering 'INJECTION ENGINE', fitted on the bootlid underneath the handle.

In view of all its qualities, the vehicle was the perfect car for travel. Two special suitcases were included in the standard equipment to allow optimum use to be made of the spacious boot. Two additional suitcases were available at an extra charge; they were accommodated in the rear compartment after the rear seat bench had been folded away – and were ideal for exceptionally long journeys for driver and passenger.

Despite the technical and stylistic improvements, only 200 units were produced of all three bodywork versions of the 300 Sc Coupé. From early 1957, the customers' interest in this model and its sister models began to dwindle, so production of the 300 Sc was discontinued in April 1958. This decline was to a certain extent attributable to the launch of the 300 SL Roadster, which was obviously the more attractive offer for many prospective buyers, being as much as 4,000 Deutschmarks less expensive despite its more contemporary styling and higher performance.

With total production figures of just 314 units between the two versions – 300 S Coupé and the 300 Sc Coupé – these rank among the most exclusive Mercedes-Benz passenger car models of the post-war period. The legendary 300 S Coupé was considered one of the finest 'Luxo-Coupés' of its day and as such was among the most highly coveted Benzes of all time.

THE PONTON BODY COUPÉ

The 220 S Coupé (W180 II), 1956–9

In March 1956, a new 220 model was presented, this time with a modern integral Ponton body (also known as the

The beautiful lines of the new 220 Coupé, showing the integrated body. The only sign of wings now was a chrome outline.

'Sindelfingen body', in reference to where it was built), which was firmly welded to the bottom of the framework. It was based upon the 180 model, which had been produced for six months by then. The 6-cylinder model kept the internal code W180 but was referred to as model 220a. Stylistically, there was a close relationship to the previous 180 model, making it quite difficult for the layman to tell them apart. This 220 S saloon, however, became an almost instant hit and critical seller for Stuttgart.

An analysis of the design stated: 'The 220 S Coupé walks the line between traditional and modern automotive engineering. The days of the mounted wing are gone. These have now been integrated into the smooth-surfaced exterior of the body. A gently arching beading is the only visual reference to the pre-war design.'

Two months after the last 220 Convertible A had rolled off the production line in Sindelfingen, a successor, the 220 Convertible A/C, was presented at the International Motor Show in Frankfurt. Although this elegantly shaped new model was technically based mainly upon the type 220a saloon, the chassis had been shortened by 120mm (5in). The exterior of

The Mercedes-Benz type 220 SE Coupé, 1958–60, showing the folded-down rear bench seat, which provided additional space for luggage.

Although space was limited compared to the saloon version, the W180 Coupé had a full seat in the rear.

A 1950s promotional advert for the Hydrak system promoted its ease of use.

the new convertible version was completely identical with the model that had been presented at Frankfurt. A novelty, however, was the addition of the powerful 100bhp engine, as fitted to the 220 S saloon, giving the model a great boost in engine power – as well as a weight increase of 60kg (132lb) because of the required body stiffness. This convertible model, which was identical with the open version except for its fixed roof, enabled the launch of a coupé version just three months later.

In August 1957, improved versions of almost all types of the passenger car programme, including the 220 S Coupé and the convertible, were presented with the new advertising motto 'even more value at no extra cost'. They had all undergone model revision that led to slight modifications and an increased engine power of 106bhp. Visible from outside were only the changed front bumper and number plate panel as well as the modified illumination of the rear number

MERCEDES 220 S COUPÉ (W180 II)

Engine	Front mounted, six in-line M180-111
Bore × stroke	80.5 × 72.8mm
Total displacement	2195cc
Gearing	Four-speed manual
Maximum speed	160km/h (99mph)
Rated output	100bhp at 4,800rpm; after Aug 1957, 106bhp at 5,200rpm
Drivetrain	Rear-wheel drive via Cardan shafts
Wheelbase	2,700mm (106in)
Front/rear track	1,430/1,470mm (56/58in)
Height	1,530mm (60in)
Kerb weight	1,790kg (3,946lb)
Price	DM 21,500

plate, which, as with the saloons, had been transferred to the bumper guards. What was remarkable was the new Hydrak hydraulic automatic clutch, which had also been presented in August, first as an option only for the coupé and the convertible.

Driving a Mercedes-Benz with Hydrak was an entirely new motoring experience, and a very pleasant one at that. All the advantages of shifting gears were retained, but all the work of operating a clutch pedal was eliminated. To effect a gear change, you simply moved the gear lever and the Hydrak mechanism disengaged the clutch, allowed the gear to change and engaged the clutch again in one smooth, continuous automatic operation. Gear changing could be accomplished with great rapidity, yet it was impossible to stall or jerk the car, and there was no loss of acceleration or appreciable change in fuel consumption with the Hydrak system. A large brake pedal allowed left-foot braking for no-roll starts up steep gradients.

The Hydrak operating cycle was virtually instantaneous. When the gearshift lever was touched, it activated an electrical contact that opened a valve on a vacuum-operated booster unit. This in turn connected the booster with a vacuum container or suction pipe. The pressure differential, compared with atmospheric pressure, disengaged the clutch rapidly enough to permit gear changing with usual speed. After the gearshift lever was released, the vacuum side of the booster was vented by atmospheric pressure and, with the aid of pressure springs, the clutch was engaged.

MERCEDES 220 SE COUPÉ (W128)	
Engine	Front mounted, six in-line M127-1; after Aug 1959 M127-III
Bore × stroke	80 × 72.8mm
Total displacement	2195cc
Gearing	Four-speed manual
Maximum speed	160km/h (99mph)
Rated output	115bhp at 4,800rpm; after Aug 1959 120bhp at 5,200rpm
Drivetrain	Rear-wheel drive via Cardan shafts
Wheelbase	2,700mm (106in)
Front/rear track	1,430/1,470 mm (56/58in)
Height	1,530mm (60in)
Kerb weight	1,810kg (3,990lb)
Price	DM 23,400

The 220 SE Coupé (W128), 1958–60

From September 1958, both Coupé and Convertible versions were also offered as a 220 SE with fuel injection. Except for the engine, the Coupé and Convertibles were now internally code named W128.

The 2.2-litre 6-cylinder unit had a different carburation system from the well-tried engine of the 220 S, however. As

The original engine in the **W180** was the **M180/III** in carburettor form.

The new engine for the **W128** was the fuel-injected version of the **M127**.

PAUL BRACQ

Born: 13 December 1933, Bordeaux, France

Paul Bracq is a French automotive designer who is particularly
known for having worked for Mercedes-Benz, BMW, Peugeot
and Citroën. He graduated from Boulle School, where he was
a student between 1950 and 1953, and obtained a first prize
in woodcarving. As it happened, this was a solid start to his
career because it also follows the courses of the School of
Arts and Crafts and those of the school of the House of Trade
Union Bodywork.

In 1953, the monthly magazine *L'Automobile*, which devoted
several articles to first-time modellers, published two of
its best productions. Through Jean Bernard and director
of this magazine, he was quickly recruited into Philippe
Charbonneaux's design studio. This self-employed stylist
entrusted him with advertising vehicle projects, sometimes
in the form of a model with a 1:10 scale, such as the model
of the Pathé Marconi truck. He also brilliantly participated in
various bodywork projects based on Packard, Pegaso and even
Salmson.

**'*Une Nouvelle Lancia*' was the title of the article
Bracq had published in *L'Automobile* magazine,
which caught the eye of Philippe Charbonneaux.**

In 1954, Bracq was summoned to perform his military service in Germany at an army garage that just so happened to be
abundant with beautiful German cars, mostly Mercedes. Realizing that when his service was over, getting a job in his home
country with the now nearly non-existent French automobile design studios was going to be unlikely, he endeavoured to make
contact with Mercedes, which he could see had already returned to its glory of yesteryear. Surreptitiously, one day, he managed
to deposit a number of his drawings on a visit to the factory and this resulted in a ten-year contract under the direction of
Karl Wilfert at the newly
founded Advanced Styling
Unit alongside chief of
testing, Friedrich Geiger.

LA 4 CV ROSENGART   DELAHAYE - GRAND PRIX - SALON 51   CALANDRE "235"   DELAHAYE "235"

J.-P. WIMILLE

QUELQUES CRÉATIONS

PH. CHARBONNEAUX

50, RUE COPERNIC · PARIS XVI·

PASsy 81-71

While working
with the design
studio of Philippe
Charbonneaux, Bracq
participated in designs
for many automotive
manufacturers.

CAR DE PROPAGANDE DU MINISTÈRE DE L'AIR (CINEMA)   CAMION PUBLICITAIRE

Among the pieces Bracq showed Wilfert were these studies on the Mercedes-Benz sports and racing cars.

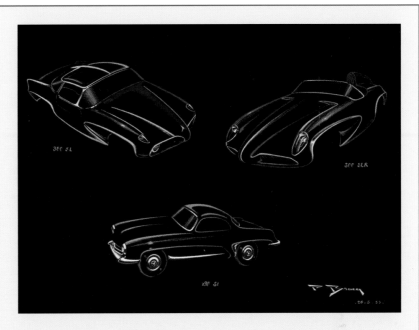

This same unit produced the W198 300 SL and created the generation of fintailed saloons W111 and 112. The symbiosis between research, style and testing provided this team with a remarkable cohesion and efficiency. For the work of modelling, the technique of using plaster, a heavy and brittle material, was quickly abandoned in favour of resin. With this, models could be made with opening doors and in which it was possible to sit. Paul Bracq remembers:

We painted the models in shiny black and placed neon tubes underneath, allowing the shadows to highlight both shape and defect. The models were returned to the modellers hundreds of times, for six months perhaps, to perfect every angle and body flow – after all it is the car bodies that define the brand and enhance their quality. The work of the chrome, for instance, was also especially important and very sophisticated. For example, for the side of the car, we had ten to fifteen sections from which to choose the one that would best take the light. The art of chrome is to optimize the part that reflects the light the versus the obscure part that is oriented towards the ground.

One of Paul's first jobs was to draw the triangular rear lights of the W110 190 saloon; then he also actively participated in the design of the 1963 W113 230 SL and the 600. He eliminated the tail fins of the previous Mercedes models, which he considered awkward-looking, too costly to manufacture and too dangerous in case of an accident.

Although in Stuttgart, all new products remained the result of teamwork, among the production vehicles he participated actively in the design of several classic cars born in 1963 – the Mercedes 220 SE and 600, the Fintails (W108, W109, W110, W111 and W112) and Strich Acht, or Stroke 8 (W114 and W115).

His first 'all-Bracq' Mercedes-Benz shapes were the W111/112 Coupé and Cabriolet launched in 1961. The C-pillar from the Fintail was retained, but the trailing-edge bend redrawn at a less acute angle. More importantly, the slightly

Where most designers at Mercedes designed in the open, Bracq preferred his own space. Drawings were pinned to every wall and filled every drawer and cupboard.

Paul Bracq's most significant contribution to Daimler-Benz was in shaping their passenger cars of the 1960s. The W108/109 was considered one of the best-looking saloons of its era.

raised wing line and reverse-cant fins were gone, replaced with a gently sloping line and forward-cant end. These shapes were a sensation, and would define the Mercedes-Benz rear for much of the 1960s.

Bracq adhered to four self-established principles in car design: well-balanced proportions, a continuous line running stem to stern along the flanks to emphasize length, wheels that fit within their well so as to appear flush with the body and a low-set waistline with deep glazed cabin above. For the W108/109 saloons of 1965, everything came together flawlessly. In retrospect, Bracq's best-looking saloon seems like a fait accompli. And so it was, but it was never just about aesthetics. Daimler-Benz was foremost a highly disciplined engineering firm and much attention was paid beyond mere styling, namely upon safety in particular.

Mercedes was an excellent school for Paul Bracq. He learned to think constantly in terms of cost, reliability, convenience and maintenance for the customer. However, after ten years in the service of Mercedes-Benz, he felt so homesick that he made the decision to return to France and take on new challenges. He worked at Brissonneau et Lotz, the renowned bodybuilder in the town of Creil. The company were also subcontractors for various car manufacturers; during Bracq's time with them, he also had a hand in the design of the body of the Matra 530 and the Opel 1900 GT. This same French coachbuilder also received several orders from BMW, which gave Bracq the opportunity to move to BMW in 1970 as director of design, where he was responsible for the design of the Series 5, Series 2, Series 3, Series 7 and, in 1973, the concept car BMW Turbo 'Studie'. This Studie later inspired the M1, Z1, 8 Series.

From 1974, Peugeot, anxious to regain some independence from Pininfarina, developed its new centre of design at Garenne Colombes and offered Paul Bracq the 'direction of the interior styling' of all it cars. Bracq became responsible for the interior design of the 305, 505, 205, 405, 106 and 406, as well as the Quasar, Proxima and Oxia concept cars.

Paul Bracq finally retired in 1996, but he never stopped drawing, painting and sculpting, with an attentive look at the achievements of brands such as Bugatti, Talbot, Facel Vega, Hotchkiss and Rolls-Royce. He is now considered one of the best contemporary automotive painters and regularly participates in exhibitions on the theme of automotive art. He is also active as a judge in several auto competitions, including the famous Pebble Beach Concours d'Elegance.

Paul Bracq standing by the author's W126 at a previous interview.

with the 300d, carburation was controlled via intermittent manifold injection, which had the effect of increasing power to 115bhp. This improvement of driving performance and better fuel consumption was only available at an extra cost of DM 1,900, however. For another DM 450 the Hydrak automatic clutch was also available as an option.

In August 1959, production of the Ponton saloons 219, 220 S and 220 SE ended, and at the same time the modified injection engine of the Type 220 SEb was used for both models, which, due to a straight intake pipe and steeper camshaft now delivered 120bhp.

The production of the Convertible and Coupé continued only in the shape of the 220 SE model, the last carburettor versions rolling off the production line in October 1959. In November 1960, production of the 220 SE stopped all together. As their successors, a new convertible was presented in February 1961 and a new coupé in August 1961. With only 5,731 units having been built, 1,942 of these with injection engine, the Ponton coupés and convertibles belong to the rarer Mercedes-Benz models of post-war production.

THE 111 AND 112 SERIES COUPÉS, 1961–71

On 24 February 1961, at the opening ceremony of the Daimler-Benz Museum in Untertürkheim, a new passenger car model, the 220 SEb Coupé, was unveiled. This elegant and representative model became the successor of the W128 series Coupé, which had gone out of production four months earlier.

From a technical and stylistic point of view, the new model was derived from the W111 220 SEb saloon, commonly referred to as the 'Fintail' model, which was presented in August 1959.

Although the Coupé and saloon still had many stylistic features in common, the prominent tail fins, which had made such a sensation at the presentation of the 220b and 220 SEb models, were now apparent only in rudimentary form. Surprisingly, at the time not a single construction element of the four-door model could be used for the Coupé, proving that Mercedes had faith in their new model.

The engine and the chassis had been taken over from the saloon without any significant modifications; however, one important difference was that the 220 SEb Coupé was the first Mercedes-Benz passenger car model to be fitted with disc brakes at the front wheels.

The sales brochure listed the key ingredients as:

Elongated, low body with racy lines, typical Mercedes-Benz radiator design, fully retractable side windows without central side posts, wide doors and high-quality interior. From whichever angle one looks at this car, you can see how the designers have striven to achieve beauty and perfection, as well as the greatest possible levels of passenger safety.

A Paul Bracq rendering of the W111 Coupé.

In contrast to its successor, the III was based upon the chassis of the saloon model, the wheelbase of which remained unchanged, accordingly making the Coupé a fully fledged four-seater model.

In August 1961, a convertible version of the 220 SEb was presented. Previously, convertible versions had generally paved the way for a coupé, but this time around a convertible was developed from the Coupé, proving that the Mercedes coupé style had found a firm place in the Mercedes line-up.

Half a year later, the 300 SE Coupé and 300 SE Convertible made their debut at the Geneva Motor Show. The bodies of the corresponding 220 SEb versions had been touched up with additional decorative elements and were combined with the technology of the 300 SE. Thus, these new exclusive models, which were, like the underlying saloon model, assigned to model series 112, featured a whole set of technical innovations. Basic equipment consisted of a 3.0-litre light-alloy engine, four-speed automatic transmission, power-brake unit, air suspension and dual-circuit brakes with disc brakes at the front and rear wheels. There was additional chrome decoration in the shape of a chrome trim extending from headlights to tail lights along the longitudinal bead as well as conspicuous decorative trims at the front and rear wheel arches.

From March 1963, the 300 SE Coupé and Convertible were, like the saloon, available with optional four-speed manual gearbox; in this case the list price was reduced by DM 1,400. In January 1964, engine power was increased to 170bhp so that driving performance was improved. This was made possible by converting the injection pump into a six-plunger unit.

BATTISTA (PININ) FARINA

Born: 2 November 1893, Cortanze, Italy
Died: 3 April 1966, Lausanne, Switzerland

Battista (Pinin) Farina.

When Farina was born in 1893, he was the tenth of his parents' eleven children. He came to be named 'Pinin', the equivalent of 'baby' in the Piedmontese dialect that his parents, natives of Cortanze d'Asti, spoke in the household.

An elder brother, Giovanni, apprenticed with a Turin coachbuilder and, in 1910, Pinin and Giovanni joined up with another brother, Carlo, to form their own business, calling it Stabilimenti Farina.

Barely out of his teens, the young Farina was supervising construction of World War I aircraft for Italy. He found himself in a privileged position, moving in the circles of many key figures of early automotive history. The Agnelli family asked him to create a prototype for Fiat called the Zero, and his immediate love of motor racing and his unexpectedly strong talent for driving turned the gifted head of Vincenzo Lancia.

In 1920, enthralled by the budding American car industry, Battista travelled to Detroit to meet industry titan Henry Ford. Ford was so impressed with the

27-year-old that he offered him a job on the spot. Battista was flattered by the offer but chose instead to return to Italy, inspired by the dynamism of Ford and the flourishing US auto industry.

Throughout the 1920s, Battista continued to work on and drive innovative designs at his brother's shop to feed his passion for fast and beautiful automobiles. Battista won the 1921 Aosta–Gran San Bernardo race in his own car, setting a track record that went unbroken for eleven years. At these tracks, Battista met future colleague Enzo Ferrari. In 1930, Battista founded Carrozzeria Pinin Farina, using his nickname to put his stamp on the auto industry. Before long, his company was producing seven or eight car bodies a day. In the 1930s, Carrozzeria Pinin Farina established relationships with GM and Renault and earned international acclaim.

The studio quickly developed a good reputation for close-coupled saloons, but even in a war-shortened decade, Pinin Farina also created some astonishing streamlined cars, usually on Alfa or Lancia Astura chassis. World War II was a difficult time, but once these clouds cleared, Battista was producing again. His most famous car in this period was the 1946 Cisitalia Coupé.

The 1946 Cisitalia Coupé.

In the year or so before it appeared, Pinin Farina had already created coupé and sports convertible bodies of relatively similar dimension on chassis sourced from Alfa, Maserati and even the plebeian Fiat 1500. The swerve proved that Farina understood that his company's future would be underpinned by design work from auto makers, not wealthy individual car owners.

Farina's fabled alliance with Ferrari dates to 1952. His first creation was a convertible on a 212 Inter chassis, but his palettes were far more varied, including not just the Nash-Healey, but the Nash sedans that Inspector Henderson drove in *The Adventures of Superman*.

Longer-term acclaim went to the lovely little Giulietta Spider from Alfa Romeo, a theme that is still gently reflected in some of Alfa's much newer cars.

Forever the family man, Battista entrusted his company and his life's work to his son, Sergio 'Pinin' Farina, and his son-in-law, Renzo Carli, upon his retirement in 1961. That same year, the Italian government authorized the change of Battista's last name from Farina to Pininfarina as a symbol of gratitude for his contributions as a torch-bearer for the Italian auto industry.

His final personal piece of design work, before he died in 1966, was the Alfa Romeo Duetto.

He was posthumously inducted into the Automotive Hall of Fame in 2004, Sergio accepting his father's award on behalf of the Pininfarina family.

With the 220 SEb, for the first time a convertible was derived from the coupé shape and not the saloon.

Nothing more is known about the whereabouts and subsequent fate of this very interesting 300 SE Coupé.

In 1962 the test department also constructed an individual special design of the 300 SE Coupé. The rear roof edge was removed, together with the rear window, and replaced by a retractable hood. This resulted in a landaulet, which for several years became the personal car of Professor Nallinger, head of the development department. Nothing more is known about the whereabouts and subsequent fate of this interesting car.

When the Fintail saloons of models 220 Sb, 220 SEb and 300 SE were replaced by a completely reconstructed generation of models, the coupé and convertible versions remained in the sales programme. As these exclusive models, which had been produced for some years by then, were by no means outdated beside the saloons of the new generation, expensive stylistic revision, or the development of new small-scale serial production of model versions, were unnecessary. The two 2.2-litre models received the 150bhp 2.5-litre engine of the 250 SE and its model designation. Furthermore, like the 3.0-litre models, they were fitted with the 14in wheels and bigger disc brakes of the 108 series saloons. New, too, was the hydropneumatic compensating spring at the rear axle, which had been incorporated into the

The new hydropneumatic suspension system was initially applied to the rear wheels only, but later on the 300 SE also at the front.

MERCEDES-BENZ W111 AIR SUSPENSION SYSTEM

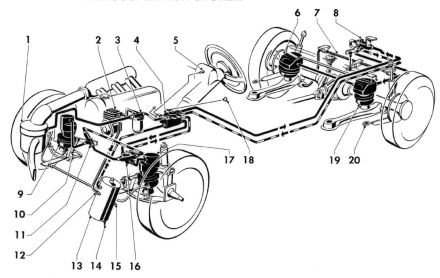

1. Air Filter	6. Air Chamber	11. Level Compensator	16. Level Compensator
2. Air Compressor	7. Torsion Bar	12. Check Valve	17. Air Chamber
3. Frost protection	8. Level Compensator	13. Reservoir	18. Pull Switch
4. Valve Unit	9. Air Bellows	14. Drain Valve	19. Air Bellows
5. Warning Light	10. Regulator Arm	15. Fill Valve	20. Brake Support

2.5-litre models instead of the coil spring that had hitherto been used, guaranteeing that the level of the body remained constant, irrespective of loads.

January 1968 witnessed the debut of the 280 SE model, which had a newly developed 2.8-litre engine with 160bhp and became the successor of the 250 SE. This change of generation did not only affect the saloon, but also the two-door versions. Apart from the new engine, only some details had been changed in the Coupé and the Convertible; like the saloon, both received flatter one-piece decorative wheel covers with integrated boss cap. At the same time as the 2.5-litre models, production of the 300 SE Coupé and Convertible was stopped. There was no immediate successor, but this was not necessary either, as engine power was only 10bhp lower than in the 2.8-litre versions and the same driving performance was achieved because of their lower weight.

In September 1969, the more powerful 280 SE 3.5 Coupé and Convertible were presented. The completely new 3.5-litre V8-engine with 200bhp was noticeably quiet and smooth and made for a much sportier feel. These new models, and the 280 versions with the 2.8-litre 6-cylinder engine, also had minor external modifications. The radiator grille was lower and wider, and accordingly the bonnet was lower at the front. The bumpers were also slightly modified, now

The new M116 V8 engine.

being fitted with rubber strips, like on the saloons. There were no external differences between the 8-cylinder versions and the new 6-cylinder versions.

In May 1971, the production of the 2.8-litre Coupé and Convertible ended, followed by the 8-cylinder version two months later. This not only brought the 111 and 112 series Coupés and Convertible to an end but also ended the high-class saloon coupé concept; from February 1972, the C107 became the successor of the coupé models. This car was no longer based on a saloon, however, but on the SL R107 model, which had been launched in April 1971. No replacement was planned for the saloon convertibles either – Mercedes drivers had to be content with the two-seater SL.

A total of 28,918 Coupés in this range were built in Sindelfingen:

220 SEb Coupé	14,173
250 SE Coupé	5,259
300 SE Coupé	2,419
280 SE Coupé	3,797
280 SE 3.5 Coupé	3,270

THE PININFARINA SPECIAL ONE-OFF COUPÉ

The story begins in 1951 with the introduction of the W186, a hand-built, separate chassis marque flagship. The 300 saloon, built in various derivations from 1951 to 1957, was aimed at wealthy industrialists and heads of state; indeed, it was nicknamed in honour of one – West Germany's post-hostilities chancellor, Konrad Adenauer, who presided over the country's remarkable Marshall Plan-assisted economic recovery.

When Pininfarina indicated to Mercedes in late 1954 their desire to purchase a 300 B to be rebodied as a pillarless coupé, the typically fastidious Germans – wary of a design that could prove detrimental to the firm's standards – requested renderings of the proposed design. Once satisfied with this, Mercedes shipped chassis #186.010 450005, a 1954 300 B, to F.A. Saporiti, the Mercedes-Benz dealer in Milan, on 17 January 1955.

Pininfarina's styling of this unique Mercedes-Benz 300 B Coupé is a blend of other cars of the period, with hints of Facel Vega, Bentley and Pininfarina's later Lancia Flaminia Coupé. This 300 B is one of only three Pininfarina-bodied Mercedes-Benz cars built in the mid-1950s, each with a distinctively different body.

In 1956, Pininfarina once more set themselves the task of converting a 300, this time turning their attention to the short-chassis, more powerful 300 SC model, which employed a more lightly tuned version of the 300 SL's 6-cylinder unit. This time, the more close-coupled style was mated to a more upright grille treatment, a lower, more enclosed roof line and canopy, and more considered use of brightwork.

The 300 S was Daimler-Benz AG's luxury flagship of the post-war era, with its flowing wings and dignified Sindelfingen coachwork influenced by pre-war tradition. The Pininfarina 300s pre-empted the look that Mercedes-Benz adopted when the 220 S Coupé was introduced for 1957.

It remains an important example of the occasional collaboration between Pininfarina and Mercedes-Benz and a particularly memorable one-off.

The original Pininfarina 300 B version with hints of Facel Vega and Bentley.

PIETRO FRUA

Born: 2 May 1913, Turin, Italy
Died: 28 June 1983

After training as a technical draftsman at the Fiat vocational school Stabilimenti Farina, Frua's professional career began at the age of seventeen as an assistant draftsman at the then leading Turin bodywork design company. At the age of twenty-two, in 1935, he was promoted to chief draftsman, and in 1941 he finally went into business for himself.

Frua designed and built more than 230 car body creations as one-offs, prototypes, small and large series vehicles on the mechanics of almost all major car manufacturers in Europe. These included AC, Alfa Romeo, BMW, Borgward, Citroën, DB/Panhard, Fiat, Ford, Glas, Jaguar, Lancia, Maserati, MG, Lamborghini, Opel, OSCA, Peugeot, Renault, Rolls-Royce, Volkswagen and Volvo.

Pietro Frua was one of the great freelance body designers at the 'Scuola Italiana', who founded the 'Italian Line' in the 1950s. His projects were created, in the same way an artist would draw or paint,

Pietro Frua.

as an expression of his personal taste and experience, although in the four decades (1935–1979), Frua adapted his designs to follow current fashions, technical developments, and the wishes of its customers. Influences of many of his Italian Line colleagues can be seen in his work and vice versa too. He would often reuse or reinvent his own design elements.

His contributions to automobile design were significant, but he never got the public recognition he deserved. His quiet and humble demeanour may have contributed to this. Nevertheless, the British weekly *Picture Post* referred to him as 'among the "Fashion Kings of the Car World"', while the German news magazine *Der Spiegel* said, 'He belongs in the same group as the most important carrozzieri of the early 1960s: Nuccio Bertone, Carrozzeria Ghia, Giovanni Michelotti, Giovanni Battista Pininfarina, Alfredo Vignale and Ugo Zagato.' Rino Sanders wrote in the weekly newspaper *Die Zeit* in 1968: 'Turin determines what is modern in the international motoring world to an unbelievable degree. Pininfarina, Bertone, Ghia, Frua, Vignale – these are names known like Dior, Cardin, Chanel, Courrèges.'

Frua has a place in this book due to his passion for the coupé automobile and his attempt at a redesign of the W113 into a coupé shooting brake, unusually incorporating the saloon grille into the nose.

The forward thinking Pininfarina design of the 300s did away with the original flowing wings and hinted at what future models would look like.

The car was powered by a 2996cc in-line 6-cylinder engine offering 123bhp. There was a four-speed manual gearbox and four-wheel vacuum-assisted hydraulic drum brakes.

MERCEDES-BENZ FRUA 230 SLX SHOOTING BRAKE COUPÉ (1966)

This little-known coupé, the W113, was commissioned by the Viazzo family of Geneva and was based upon a 1964 230 SL.

It was delivered to Switzerland in June of 1966. Very little is known about this vehicle, but it was sold on to Javier Ruperez, a politician and diplomat at the Spanish embassy in Geneva in December of the same year. He re-registered it in Madrid in March 1984.

THE 600 (W100)

The presentation of the 600 model at the International Motor Show in Frankfurt created a real sensation. Since the new top model had been designed as an exclusive representative car, intended to fulfil the highest demands, it was equipped with many new technical details, which, taken together, stood for the highest standard that could be achieved in technological terms at the time.

For the first time in the history of Daimler-Benz, a V8 injection engine was used, which delivered maximum power of 250bhp from a 6.3-litre cubic capacity and around 500Nm (369lb ft) of torque. With the standard automatic transmission, this car achieved a driving performance more typical of a sports car. The 600 model, weighing almost 2.5 tons, reached a maximum speed of 205km/h (127mph) and accelerated from 0 to 100km/h in 10 seconds.

Shock absorbers that could be adjusted at the steering column during the ride as well as air-pressure-supported

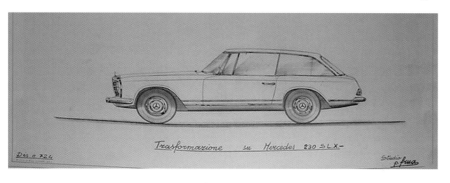

A rare design drawing of the 230 SLX shooting brake.

FRUA 230 SLX SHOOTING BRAKE SPECIFICATION

Base vehicle	Mercedes-Benz 230 SL (W113.042), chassis #113.042-10-008218
Engine type	M127.11
Bore × stroke	82 × 72.8mm
Compression ratio	9.5:1
Total displacement	2306cc
Rated output	150bhp (110kW) at 5,500rpm
Transmission	Single-disc dry clutch, four-speed toothed thrust transmission with a centre shift lever, Cardan shaft, rear-wheel drive
Front axle	Independent wheel suspension with double triangular wishbones, coil springs, telescopic shock absorbers and stabilizer; recirculating ball steering
Rear axle	Single-joint swing axle, coil springs and telescopic shock absorbers
Brakes	Hydraulically operated disc brakes at the front and drum brakes at the rear
Top speed	195–200km/h (121–4mph)
Acceleration	0–100km/h: 11sec

dual-circuit brakes offered maximum safety. All four wheels were equipped with disc brakes. The front wheels had moreover been fitted with two double-jaw brakes each.

The extremely generous basic equipment of the 600 model – air suspension, power brakes, central locking systems and an electronic heating and airing system – afforded a maximum of ride comfort and easy handling. Unique hydraulics for extra comfort ensured automatic operation of the following functions: horizontal and vertical adjustment of the front seats, inclination control of the back of the seat, adjustment of the rear seats in a longitudinal direction, and opening and closing of the vehicle doors, the boot lid, the optional sliding sunroof and the side windows.

Series production of this 'Grand Mercedes' began in September 1964. Apart from a five-/six-seater saloon with 3,200mm (126in) wheelbase, there were three seven- and eight-seater Pullman versions with 3,900mm (154in) wheelbase available: a four-door Pullman limousine with rear seating in a face-to-face arrangement,

a six-door Pullman limousine with rear seats and additional folding tables in driving direction, and the Pullman landaulet. The last was available in four different versions. The standard version had four doors, rear seating in a face-to-

The W113 on a publicity shoot.

face arrangement and a hood reaching to the front edges of the rear doors. As a special design, a six-door version with rear seats and additional fold-down chairs in driving direction was also available. As with the six-door Pullman limousine, the doors in the middle could also be ordered without handles. As landaulets, both the four-door and the six-door version were available with an extra-long hood, which extended as far as the middle partition.

The short-wheelbase W100 600.

The 600 used the new M100 engine, the first time that any saloon Mercedes had a V8 engine. It was 'dry sump' to limit height.

THE 600 COUPÉ

Mercedes-Benz experimented with a two-door version of the iconic 600 (W100) in the middle of the 1960s as a simple 'design study'. While the existing long- and short-wheelbase four-door models were largely aimed at buyers who had a chauffeur, the 600 Coupé was intended to capture the top end of the personal luxury car market.

Save for a set of air vents mounted directly behind the front wheels, the 600 Coupé closely resembled its four-door counterpart from the tip of the front bumper to the A-pillar. Beyond that, the wheelbase was shortened to 2,980mm (117in) – bringing the car's total length to 5,320mm (209in) while still retaining the angular roofline. The rear end was again essentially identical to that of the saloon, and a set of 15in steel wheels covered by chromed hubcaps created a look of understated elegance.

Inside, the dashboard, the steering wheel, the stalks and switches and the instrument cluster were all carried over from the standard 600. The front seatbacks tilted forward to provide easy access to a bench seat that could accommodate up to three adults, and the rear windows were powered by the same hydraulic system as the saloon versions. A smooth, comfortable ride was assured by an advanced air suspension system.

Under the bonnet the Coupé remained the same as the saloon versions as well, powered by the fuel-injected M 100 6.3-

Initially only built as a design study, the 600 Coupé was a beautifully balanced vehicle. It caused many internal arguments as to whether it should be offered.

As a nod to the prestigious landaulet carriages, the W600 was also offered with a foldable tonneau cover at the rear.

The 600 Coupé's interior was as well equipped as any saloon version and, due to its overall size, there was ample space in the rear to accommodate three adults.

litre V8 engine. This was more than enough to propel the 2,450kg (5,401lb) Coupé from zero to 100km/h in a respectable 9.7 seconds with two occupants on board. The top speed of 205 km/h (127mph) was the same as the saloon.

For reasons that remain unclear, Mercedes decided to allocate its resources to other projects and the company's records indicate that only two 600 Coupés were built in August of 1965, neither of which went up for sale: they were presented to engineers Rudolf Uhlenhaut and Fritz Nallinger as retirement gifts. One of the cars was sold by the Nallinger family and is now part of a private collection, but the other's whereabouts remain unknown.

MERCEDES-BENZ CONCEPT COUPÉ

At the 1993 Geneva Motor Show, Mercedes-Benz presented a concept coupé that would eventually mark the opening shot in what was to become a new product drive. The dynamic design language, even though only in concept

A couple of early designs of the 'four-eyed' coupé concept by Ingo Feuerherdt (top) and Michel Fink (bottom).

The 1993
Geneva
concept coupé
kept the rear
appointments
drawn by Fink
and the front
of Feuerherdt.

The Geneva concept car was intended to test the waters and ask the question of how customers would react to a new four-seater Mercedes-Benz coupé to replace the C127. The immediate excitement and follow-up interest received by Daimler proved that the coupé remained a viable option.

form, gave a foretaste of many themes that would later be taken up by Mercedes models.

The most immediately noticeable feature of the coupé concept was the introduction to the world of the 'four-eyes headlamp', a design that would later become the new face of the brand. The response from both the press and the public was overwhelmingly positive and that meant a thumbs-up for production. The first model in which the new front-end design hit the road was also one of the brand's most important models: the all-new four-headlamp W210 E-Class, which appeared in 1995.

The concept coupé was not just a show car but fully drivable. Under the bonnet was an 8-cylinder 5.0-litre engine developing maximum power of 235kW (320bhp) and maximum torque of 470Nm (347lb ft) at 3,900rpm. This too was a taste of things to come, portending the future CLK 500. The coupé also showed careful attention to practical requirements. Interestingly, although the coupé concept shown in Geneva did have a tail section, albeit short-cropped, it did not have a conventional bootlid. In its place was a large tailgate that incorporated the rear

screen and extended down as far as the edge of the bumper, making this the first ever Mercedes-Benz fastback. It had an ample 485ltr (128gal) capacity too. This innovative tailgate became a defining styling feature with the 2000 C203 C-Class Coupé.

The concept car came with a totally unrealistic glass roof that continued almost seamlessly into the tailgate, but it did have a fully functional interior too.

The elegance of the exterior continued uninterrupted into an interior, with four single, individual seats. Here the emphasis was on fluency of form and an absence of frills. The centre console, running all the way through from the dashboard to the parcel shelf, was a key design element. Smooth leather, luxurious microfibre fleece and wood panelling created a driving environment that was refined and elegant. At the same time, the ergonomics were designed to the high standards for which Mercedes-Benz is renowned. This could be seen, for example, in the front seats with their asymmetrical head restraint mounting. These 'ergonomic wing' seats offered excellent lateral and spinal support even at shoulder level.

The concept came with what was believed to be a gimmick – its glass roof – but this is something that has come to fruition in recent years. The interior (inset) was fully functional.

Bruno Sacco said, 'We don't go in for quirky show cars with pointless special effects. Such cars may cause a stir briefly but they are usually forgotten within the space of a few motor shows,' and this coupé contributed to so many subsequent production models that his dictum proved to be just as true of a concept model.

As a recap, the 'four-headlamp' design appeared in the following models:

CLK (W208, W209, C208, C209, A208, A209)
C-Class (W203, CL203, S203)
CL (C215)
SL (R230)

Highlights of it were:

Four-eye face: introduced in 1995 in the E-Class (W210)
Fastback tail: introduced in 2000 in the C-Class Sports Coupé (CL203)
Grey-tinted all-glass roof: introduced in 2002 in the E-Class (W211)
Step-in light
Front seats with asymmetrical head restraint mounting ('ergo wing' seats)

MAYBACH EXELERO

Although not strictly a Mercedes-Benz saloon coupé, the Exelero has been included here as Maybach's parent company is Daimler and the vehicle was derived from Mercedes-Benz parts and design.

High-Speed Tyre Safety Testing

In 1933, after large parts of the revolutionary autobahn motorway system had been completed, it became possible for the first time to maintain high speeds over long distances and for long periods of time. The tyre industry was required to take these new conditions into account with high-performance and hard-wearing products.

Tyre maker Fulda recognized the signs of the time and started planning for a test car with the focus of attention on maximum speed. The objective was to break the 'speed barrier' of 200km/h (124mph), at that time an incredible speed and one in which aerodynamics proved to be an important factor.

Based on preliminary discussions, the Maybach chassis quickly became the logical favourite among those automobile designs considered, not least because the engines offered remarkable performance. Furthermore, close business relations already existed between the two companies, as Fulda had previously been involved as an OEM tyre supplier for Maybach cars.

In researching the 100th anniversary, drawings and photos were discovered of the Maybach streamlined vehicle SW38 from 1938, which had been commissioned by Fulda.

The documents revealed that, at the end of the 1930s, Fulda requested renowned Frankfurt coachbuilders Dörr and Schreck to develop a car with streamlined bodywork for the purpose of high-speed tyre testing.

The background to this ambitious project was an important boost to development in vehicle manufacturing and in the development of the road network. The 1930s revolutionized the process of automobile manufacturing and Fulda had played no small part in this upswing.

Similarly, Dunlop had also commissioned a streamlined vehicle from Daimler-Benz, who used a rebodied W29, 540K, for exactly the same reason – to high-speed test the durability of its tyres.

Spohn Karosserie Ravensburg had already collaborated with Maybach and produced streamlined versions of a number of his cars, especially the 'Zeppelin' model, so the first design of the special-purpose vehicle was based on this; however, with its 12-cylinder engine, it was deemed too heavy and, in the end, the smaller 6-cylinder, 3.6-litre, 140bhp Maybach SW38 was chosen.

Fulda and Maybach commissioned aerodynamics specialist Freiherr Reinhard Koenig Fachsenfeld to develop the legendary Fulda Maybach streamlined car and the well-known German aerodynamic expert did not disappoint. Not only was a streamlined masterpiece created, but it was one of the first automobiles designed specifically to create an undisturbed airflow at the rear end of the vehicle. The aerodynamic studies conducted on the car were done in a wind tunnel using wool threads attached to numerous parts of the bodywork so the designers could visualize what was happening at a microscopic level. It achieved a sensational maximum speed of over 200km/h (124mph).

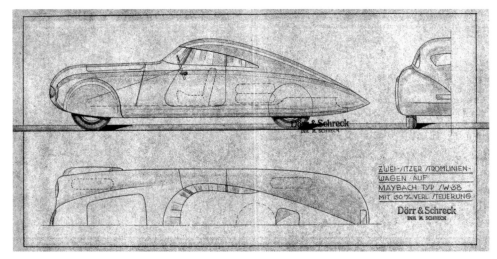

Coachbuilders Dörr and Schreck penned the design for Maybach and Fulda.

The vehicle was completed on 27 July 1939. The delivery of this unique special vehicle was followed with great interest by the experts and the specialist press. Due to the start of World War II, however, it was no longer possible to use the Maybach on the planned scale. Within a few months the streamlined car had disappeared as the world plunged into global war, never to be seen again.

The Return of the Fulda Maybach

Some sixty-seven years after completion of the famous streamlined automobile, the May-bach and Fulda companies stood together in the public limelight once again. To be clear, the new vehicle was neither a reprise of the original, nor a retro design from the last century. The astonishing result of the 2005 collaboration was indeed an unmistakable tribute to its predecessor, but also a high-tech highlight of an incredibly special kind.

With the intention of projecting a piece of history into the future through the modern interpretation of the streamlined car of 1938, several creative minds were assembled in the project team for the new Fulda Maybach Concept Car. Commissioned to create a fascinating blend of strength and elegance, the Pforzheim Polytechnic's design department and the design department of DaimlerChrysler AG set the co-operative relationship, which had operated successfully for many years, into motion once again.

A considerable planning effort and meticulous detailed work dominated the daily round of the team meetings during the first few months. For the four students at the college's transport design department, the work on the design of the unique vehicle represented an unforgettable challenge. Under the guidance of Wolf Seebers, their aim was to achieve the best possible combination of elegance and high performance. In particular, the contours of the radiator grille clearly indicate the inspiration of the characteristic Maybach design. The line from the cockpit to the tail section, in contrast, was designed in two steps that bear a close resemblance to the design style of Formula 1.

Andreas Hellmann's proposed design went in another

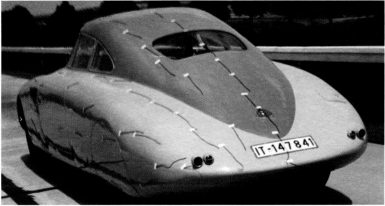

Freiherr Reinhard Koenig created a stunning streamlined car that could reach speeds in excess of 200km/h (124mph).

direction. His concept had a very American look about it but, at the same time, possessed unmistakable traces of its historic predecessor. The choice of two-colour paintwork, for example, is an attractive visual reference to the famous test vehicle from 1939.

Like the model from Andreas Hellmann, the design study from Stefan Barth also called for a two-colour paint job for the new concept car. The design of the tail unit was based on the model of a boat's stern. The most striking modification in Barth's concept was that the fins on the hood of the original were extended harmoniously into the line of the roof.

The design study by Fredrik Burchhardt led to different associations: while some recognized significant traces of a Corvette split window, others drew comparisons with the construction of a catamaran. The design, in the colours red and black, put the focus clearly on the radiator

The Exelero was built to emulate the design cues of the original W38.

grille and deliberately avoided the use of a fender at the front.

Initially, it was Fredrik Burchhardt's design that emerged as the winner, but the outstanding creative efforts of Barth, Hellmann and Seebers were not ignored in the following implementation phase.

All four designs were milled as 1:4 models and from each of the presented designs, important ideas and impulses were picked up and incorporated into an exceptional design of an incomparable vehicle.

As outstanding as the concept designs were, their implementation was equally professional and exclusive and was the result a masterly arrangement of the most striking style elements of limousine and coupé, combined in a spectacular sports car based on the Maybach 57.

The completion of the Fulda Maybach Concept Car appears more remarkable when one considers the challenging objective of developing a coupé based on an existing limousine without creating a completely new design. Despite a tight time schedule, Jürgen Weissinger, the responsible project engineer and manager of development at Maybach, together with his team managed to realize the project successfully.

The sports coupé took shape at the end of May 2004: after three model phases had been successfully completed, the exterior, interior and chassis were tested, adapted, and perfected. In the 1:1 model, dreams, visions and ideas took on concrete form in the final reference object for the decisive step in development: the construction and test process.

**Four designers were asked to participate
on the design of the Exelero.**

Wolf Seebers · Andreas Hellmann

Stefan Bath · Fredrik Burchhardt

However, with the reinterpretation of the stream-lined car of 1938, it was not only intended to create an optical novelty of modern automobile manufacturing. The targeted 350km/h (217mph) maximum speed confronted the commissioned design engineers with the challenge of manufacturing a fully functional special vehicle, which, as the fastest Maybach ever, would be capable of redefining the performance benchmarks for limousines on standard tyres.

However, it quickly became clear that, despite the Biturbo boost, the original 12-cylinder engine would not be able to

The flow of lines from front to rear give the impression of speed, even while standing still.

There are clear design cues from the original Maybach 38 Zeppelin, especially the raked radiator grille.

produce the targeted maximum speed. The vitally necessary assistance came from Untertürkheim. The specialists in the Mercedes Car Group optimized the turbocharger and increased the cubic capacity of the type 12 engine to 5.9 litres. In the end, 700bhp of engine output confirmed the technological brilliance of the implemented modifications.

For this model, a tyre was designed that not only coped with the above-mentioned weight, dimensions and speed, but also gave the car safety, stability and comfort. The alloy wheels of the Exelero are 23in diameter at both front and

rear. The tyres are Fulda Carat Exeleros, sized as 315/25 ZR23, which were the specific tyres to be tested and which spurred on the creation of the Exelero. The final result was more than convincing: on 1 May 2005, racing driver Klaus Ludwig drove the Maybach Exelero, fitted with Fulda tyres, in Nardo in Italy and attained a speed of 351.45km/h (218.38mph) – setting a new world speed record for limousines on series-production tyres.

The Maybach Exelero was not just a sporty test car, it combined the elegance and first-class quality of a high-end limousine with the silky-smooth power of a sports

Even from the rear, the Exelero gives an impression of movement.

Most materials used in the car's interior are dark and red leather. The car contains carbon-fibre and aluminium accents, creating a luxurious and sporty look that has red harness-style seatbelts for added flair.

MAYBACH EXELERO SPECIFICATION

Engine type	Turbocharged petrol	Length	5,890mm (232in)
Cylinders	V12 in 60-degree V	Width	2,140mm (84in)
Capacity	5908cc (360.528cu in)	Height	1,390mm (55in)
Bore × stroke	83 × 91mm	Kerb weight	2,660kg (5,864lb)
Maximum power output	690bhp (515kW) at 5,000rpm	Fuel capacity	110ltr (24.2gal)
Maximum torque	1,020Nm (752ft lb) at 2,500rpm	Maximum speed	351km/h (218mph)
Wheelbase	3,390mm (133in)	Acceleration	0–100km/h: 4.4sec

coupé. It is a car that attained a top speed of over 350km/h (217mph) with an unladen weight of 2.66 tons and the dimensions of a small van.

Rapper Jay-Z used the car in one of his music videos ('Lost One', 2006) and so smitten was he that he asked to buy it. It cost him a princely US$8 million.

CHAPTER EIGHT

THE INTERMEDIATE CLASS SALOON

With the introduction of the 'New Generation' of Mercedes automobiles, a new position was found for the coupé. Commencing with the R107 SL range, the coupé became the 'Sport-Light Coupé', both as an alternative to a fully convertible sports car and as a 'sporting' addition to the S-Class range – although following the SL range by featuring the SL-style sports grille.

There remained room, however, for a 'coupé in all classes', as it was referred to by Daimler in their advertising, and so the 'intermediate class coupé' was born.

Under the auspices of Dr Fritz Nallinger, Mercedes-Benz chief engineer, member of the board of management and technical director of Daimler-Benz AG, designers and engineers began planning the new model series as early as 1961, the same year the W110 Fintail reached the market.

The technical structure of the forthcoming vehicle was determined by Karl Wilfert, head of body development. It was very clear at the beginning of development that this new intermediate class had to be an independent, successful model and that the shared body was no longer an option. Stuttgart therefore endeavoured to create a complement to the new luxury class 108/109 series for the year 1968.

As far back as 1960, chief engineer Nallinger defined important benchmarks for the new vehicle. In direct comparison with the luxury class model, the design was to be appreciably more compact than differences between the 4- and 6-cylinder variants of the shared body allowed. In view of the smaller exterior dimensions, it would be important to ensure good space economy in the passenger compart-

The W108/W109 was launched to the press on the day before it premiered at the Frankfurt Auto Show in 1965.

Paul Bracq explained in his book *Carrosserie Passion* that: 'The elegance of the rear pillar did not satisfy anyone, least of all Karl Wilfert, "the boss". Finally one day, a bit tired of looking for the "impossible", I simply copied a Cadillac rear quarter-panel and that little trick was able to charm the whole board.'

Reminiscent of the BMW 'Hofmeister kink', this design displeased Karl Wilfert enormously.

Finally, in early 1965, a decision was made to refrain from such differentiation, as seen in the two model series 115 and 114 later. This was the year in which Professor Dr Hans Scherenberg took over project management as chief engineer when Nallinger went into retirement.

Other body variants developed in addition to the saloon were a coupé, a long-wheelbase saloon and a station wagon. Whereas the sportier two-door and the long-wheelbase version of the saloon actually made it into production, the station wagon was ultimately barred from series production. Nevertheless, the basic design of the rear end was later harmoniously transferred to the next model series, the 123, with only minor changes. In 1967, the production facilities for the new series were set up in Sindelfingen. Prior to the market launch proper, 1,100 pre-production vehicles of the two series were produced there, limited initially to six models.

THE 'STROKE 8'

The Stroke 8 made its public debut at the beginning of 1968 with six saloon models. Over the course of its career, its outstanding qualities meant that it shaped a whole generation of automobiles; today, it has not only become an established classic but has defined a generation of Mercedes. The name 'Stroke 8' refers to the year of its official premiere, 1968.

The models consisted of a 200 and 220, which were powered by the new 4-cylinder M115 carburettor engine, with 2-litre displacement (70kW/95bhp) and 2.2-litre displacement (77kW/105bhp) respectively. The 200 D and 220 D diesel variants also featured a new engine, the OM615, in a 2-litre version with 40kW (55bhp) and a 2.2-litre variant with 44kW (60bhp) output. The 2.3-litre in-line 6-cylinder M180 engine of the 230 model was already familiar from the predecessor model; it developed 88kW (120bhp), as in the W110. New in the

ment. The shape had to be timeless in its simple elegance. In 1964, the designers' models already showed the outlines of the future saloon. At that point, however, different designs of the front end were still under discussion. Again, in a clear distinction between the 4- and 6-cylinder variants, the versions of the new model family with smaller engines were to get a simpler front end with horizontally arranged rectangular headlamps.

The final design alongside the saloon in the design hall.

engine range was the 2.5-litre in-line 6-cylinder M114, which generated 96kW (130bhp).

For the new petrol engines of both series, Mercedes-Benz relied on proven technology: the 4-cylinder 200 and 220 models (M115) were fitted with Stromberg horizontal carburettors, the 6-cylinder of the 230 (M180) and 250 (M114) models with two Zenith downdraught compound carburettors. The 250 model was also equipped with an oil cooler. The in-line carburettor engines had two overhead valves per cylinder and an overhead camshaft.

The 4-cylinder power plants (petrol and diesel) proved so reliable that the 123 series that followed in 1976 was initially equipped with the M115 and OM615 engines.

The outstanding constructional detail of the new model series was to be found under the rear end; the Stroke 8 models were fitted with a so-called diagonal swing axle, making this the first Mercedes-Benz production car to have a rear axle with semi-trailing arm. The diagonal swing axle was equipped, among other things, with auxiliary rubber springs and a torsion-bar stabilizer as standard. Compared with the predecessor models, the new axle afforded distinct improvements in handling characteristics without sacrificing ride comfort. The improved handling quality was acknowledged by international motor journalists, who were invited to the old Targa Florio course in Sicily for a preliminary road test in December 1967. Snow, ice and the narrow mountain roads of the Madonie placed great demands on the suspension, but the Stroke 8 gave an excellent account of itself even though the cars were not lightweight by any means.

Wheelbase and weight of the upper mid-range series of Mercedes-Benz had grown consistently bigger from the Ponton (2,650mm/104in and 1.22 tonnes) through the W110 (2,700mm/106in and 1.28 tonnes to the Stroke

8 (2,750mm/108in and 1.36 tonnes). However, the overall length of the new model, 4,680mm (184in), was less than that of the 110 series. The new proportion of overall body length to wheelbase was also visible in silhouette, with balanced proportions and clear lines. The additional weight was due mainly to measures designed to improve passive safety, which put into practice the ideas of Mercedes-Benz engineer Béla Barényi, a pioneer in this field.

W114 SERIES COUPÉ 1968–73

From October 1968, the model line-up of the new Mercedes-Benz was rounded off at the upper end by the 250 C and 250 CE Coupé, presented to representatives of the international press who had gathered in Hockenheim. The launch of this sporty two-door was a highly regarded premiere, as this was the first time that Mercedes had offered a coupé version as an exclusive variant in the intermediate class.

Compared with the future coupé based on the E-Class, those of series 114 very closely followed the saloon in their design: neither wheelbase nor overall length differed. Starting from the A-pillar, however, the differences became

The **C114** became the first intermediate class coupé saloon of the new generation, launched in 1968.

A true 'pillarless coupé'.

The now electronically controlled Bosch D-Jetronic fuel injection was used for the very first time.

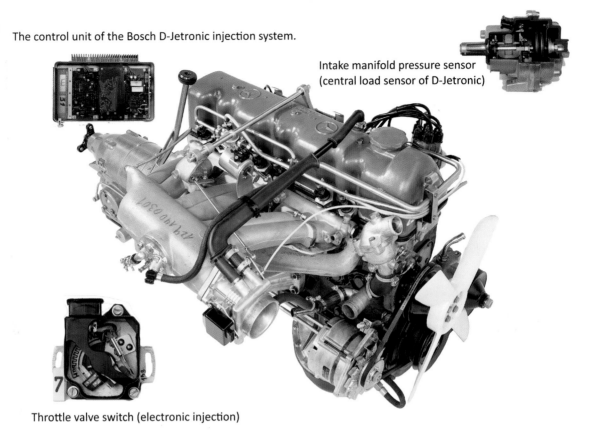

The control unit of the Bosch D-Jetronic injection system.

Intake manifold pressure sensor (central load sensor of D-Jetronic)

Throttle valve switch (electronic injection)

rather more pronounced: the Coupé had a flatter front screen and a roof that was 45mm (2in) lower compared to that of the saloon, and, of course, it was a two-door model. The front and rear side windows came without a frame and were fully retractable. Due to the missing B-pillar, an uninterrupted fresh-air zone was created in true hard-top manner. Another distinguishing feature was the longer rear bumper, which extended right up to the wheel arches and harmonized well with the long rear of the car.

The elegant sports car characteristics of the coupé were underscored by the different engine options that were available with the car. Of the two coupés, the 250 CE model proved the most exclusive in a dual sense. Apart from a 130bhp carburettor version as fitted to the saloon, a Bosch D-Jetronic fuel-injected version was used for the first time in any Mercedes-Benz production car. This electronically controlled fuel-injection system made it possible to dispense with the conventional mechanically controlled multi-plunger injection pump, increasing the power output available to 150bhp; this engine was reserved exclusively to this body type.

For press testing, Mercedes-Benz specifically chose the Hockenheimring racetrack to present its new Coupé line. Representatives from two motoring magazines, the *Motor-Rundschau* and *Auto Motor und Sport* clocked a top speed of 198km/h (123mph) for the 250 CE, and the *Swiss Automobile Revue* magazine, from Bern, even measured 199km/h (124mph). The car thus almost reached the magical mark of 200km/h (124mph), which was still outstanding for passenger cars at the time.

The experts were equally impressed by the sporty design and high-quality interior features – the fine wood veneer in the instrument panel, for example, and carpeting. Trade magazine *Auto Motor und Sport* commented after running a test: 'The Coupé also provides the level of comfort missing from the saloon. A touch of luxury is offered in a functional package at an acceptable price.'

In April 1972 the 280 and 280 E models were added to the range. Both were available in saloon form or as a coupé and were powered by the newly designed 2.8-litre M110 engine. The 6-cylinder had overhead valves in a V configuration and two overhead camshafts. In the carburettor version

The newly designed M110 straight-six twin-cam engine became the new top-of-the-line model 280 C.

it developed 118kW (160bhp), and with manifold injection 136kW (185bhp). The saloons of the new top-of-the-line Stroke 8 models could be distinguished from the less powerful variants even without the model plate: in addition to the familiar double bumper of the 250, they had a rear bumper that wrapped right round to the wheel arch cutouts, as well as two tailpipes.

A technical milestone was set by the new diagonal swing axle at the rear, which significantly enhanced the Stroke 8's dynamic handling compared with its predecessor, as well as its safety. Disc brakes on all four wheels played their part in this respect, too.

On the coupé side, the 280 C model superseded the 250 CE model, production of which was discontinued. The 280 CE model, with the 136kW (185bhp) injection engine, extended the performance spectrum of the series and became the new top-of-the-range model.

With the appearance of the 280 C and 280 CE types on the market, the 250 C, too, was now fitted with a slightly detuned 130bhp version of the M110 engine, which had been carried over from the new S-Class W116 280 S. The export version of the 250C, which was destined for the United States and Canada, had been fitted with this engine as early as July 1969.

Facelifted W114 Series Coupé 1973–6

In September 1973, the Stroke 8 (both the Coupé and the saloons) underwent a model revision; numerous details, which had already become part of the R107 SL and SLC types, as well as the W116 S-Class, were now introduced into the small coupé and generally enhanced car safety.

External mirrors that could be adjusted from inside the car

The various changes to the front design were narrow bumpers and a lower, wider grille.

The rain/soil-repellent rear tail lights can clearly be seen above the narrow rear bumper.

were added, along with soil-repellent decorative panels at the A-pillars, which kept the side windows clean even in poor weather conditions, profiled soil-repellent tail lights and a roof rail at the rear window. The four-spoke safety steering wheel was also introduced, having previously been used on model series 107 and 116. From March 1973, headrests and automatic safety belts in the front cabin became standard equipment too.

To bring the model recognizability in line with that of the S-Class range, the exterior, too, was upgraded. The radiator grille had been lowered and was now broader, and the number plate panel was fitted on rather than underneath the bumper. In addition, a new handle was attached to the bootlid. Moreover, the front section was redesigned to enhance resemblance to the S-Class saloons. In contrast to their saloon counterparts, the Coupés kept their swivel windows. This had the drawback, however, that the new external mirrors were not situated at the A-pillar as with the saloons, but were now placed in a somewhat unfortunate position at the rear end of the triangular windows.

Production of the small coupé ended in August 1976, over half a year after the change of generation of saloons and four months before the last Stroke 8 Mercedes had rolled off the production line. By the time production ended in August 1976, more than 67,000 units of the 114 series Coupé had

been built in just under eight years, 60 per cent of which were destined for export – the Coupé was an extremely popular variant abroad. Their successors, the 123 series Coupé models, were not to appear on the market for another eight months; standard production was launched in April 1977.

The most successful model, of which 21,787 units were built, was the 1972 250 CE.

Depending on the specific variant, a Coupé could cost up to 3,000 Deutschmarks more than a Stroke 8 saloon. For this, however, buyers got a more capacious boot, with a capacity of around 500ltr (17.7 cu ft). The two models share an air of discreet elegance, credit for which is due to the then Mercedes-Benz designer Paul Bracq, supported by Bruno Sacco.

Production figures for 1968–73:

250 C	8,824
250 C (2.8 engine)	10,527
250 CE	21,787
280 C	4,929
280 CE	7,576

Production figures for 1973–6:

250 C (2.8 engine)	1,241
280 C	8,227
280 CE	3,942

Gone was the chassis and sub-frame arrangement in favour of the completely integrated body of the 123.

W123 SERIES, 1977–85

The Saloon Variant

In January 1976, the W114/115 series, or Stroke 8, models were replaced by a totally new medium-sized range oriented to the S-Class, which had been produced for three and a half years. Its internal designation was the W123. The model family ranged from a 2.0-litre 4-cylinder diesel with 55bhp to the 2.8-litre 6-cylinder injection engine with 185bhp.

The chassis-style sub-frame of the preceding models was completely superseded by the integral body, which contributed to an even more stable security passenger cell with stiffened roof-frame structure, high-strength roof and door pillars as well as reinforced doors. The energy absorption of the deformation zone in the front and rear ends was significantly increased by a controlled deformation capacity later referred to as 'crumple zones', as patented by Béla Barényi.

All other safety-related construction details realized for the first time in series 107 and 116 were of course transferred to the medium-size types, including the new safety steering column, which appeared for the first time in series 126. Steering mechanism and steering column tube were linked together by a corrugated metal tube, which, in case of a crash, could buckle to the side: another patented invention by Barényi that severely reduced the danger of the column tube invading the interior of the car and spearing the driver.

A semi-trailing arm rear axle was carried over from the Stroke 8 models, but vast improvements of ride and stability were achieved by using a double-wishbone front suspension with zero steering offset, as premiered on the new S-Class 116.

Great steps in front and rear crumple zones had been made through extensive testing at Sindelfingen.

The Coupé Variant

Production of the 114 series Stroke 8 Coupés had run out between June and August of 1976, leaving a short delay until March 1977, when the new Coupé variant of series 123 was introduced. It was presented at the Geneva Motor Show with types 230 C, 280 C and 280 CE.

The overall design of the 123 series Coupé took its cue from the saloons. The distinctive horizontal delineation at the front and rear and the slightly wedged shape when viewed from the side; the sparing use of chrome trim; and the rounded, in the truest sense of the word, lines and wide-band headlamps gave both the Coupé and the saloons a well-balanced, dynamic shape without appearing too aggressive and, even though the wheelbase of the saloon 123 was only 65mm (2.5in) smaller than the standard W116, it succeeded in giving a more compact feel.

As in the preceding types, there was a close technical and stylistic relationship to the saloon. However, in contrast to the Stroke 8 Coupés, which were based on the standard body platform of their four-door counterpart, the wheelbase of the new two-door cars had been reduced by 85mm (3in) in comparison to the saloons. This allowed for a much less dominant tail end, thus making the coupé variant stylistically more autonomous in the range, and enabled a more homogeneous and much more attractive design.

The equipment details of the body corresponded to the upper standard of saloon version Types 280 and 280 E: thus, all three Coupé models were provided with rectangular wide-band headlamps, chromed air inlet grilles in front of the windscreen and chrome strips under the rear lamps.

Mechanically, the Coupés were exactly like their four-door counterparts. Like those, they had a semi-trailing arm

Although the C123 was pillarless like its predecessor, the side window had a chrome strip, adding to its more compact look.

The C123 retained the traditional soil-proof tail lights, and the coupé models were identifiable from the chrome strip below.

The C123 had rectangular headlights; only the North American version retained the dual round lamps due to DOT regulations.

North America initially received the OM617 diesel engine 300 D, but later this was upgraded to the OM617A turbocharged version.

5-cylinder engine, known from the saloon, made a mere 80bhp. This type was reserved for export to North America; due to the general speed limits there, thankfully no maximum speed was expected. The main reason that this unusual, almost bizarre, model was developed, however, was in order to achieve the so-called 'corporate average fuel economy', the average consumption of all Mercedes-Benz models offered in the USA. Thus, they could comply with the new consumption limit introduced by the US government. In September 1979, the performance of the OM617 5-cylinder engine could after all be raised to 88bhp through changes in the injection pump.

Two years later, in August 1981, alongside the 300 D saloon, the 300 CD was replaced by 300 CD Turbodiesel, although this remained exclusively an export to North America. This change of model was again necessary due to even more strict fleet consumption limits. To correspond to the new regulations, the export of types 280 E and 280 CE to the USA were also stopped in the model year 1982; the economic Turbodiesel, which produced only 20bhp less than the emission-controlled 2.8-litre petrol-engined car, became their successor.

However, changes in the range of engines were also seen in the petrol-powered models. In April 1978, at the same time as with the saloons, the performance of the 2.8-litre fuel-injected engines was improved to 185bhp by increasing the compression.

About two years later, in June 1980, the 2.3-litre 4-cylinder carburettor engine was replaced by a totally redeveloped engine of equal cubic capacity, the M102. It was equipped with a mechanically controlled petrol injection and achieved an additional 27bhp. Thus, the 230 C model was replaced in favour of 230 CE, which consumed around 10 per cent less fuel in spite of a performance boost of between 15 and 25 per cent. At the same time, the 280 C

rear axle, which had already been introduced in the preceding models. Furthermore, they received the double-wishbone front-wheel suspension with zero steering offset and the new braking system unchanged from the saloons.

The range of models at first consisted of types 230 C, 280 C and 280 CE. The engines corresponded exactly to the equipment of the respective saloon, but, in contrast to the preceding model, the base version of the 123 Coupé was also available with a 4-cylinder engine; its performance of 109bhp was adequate rather than overwhelming in power.

Engine Changes

The diesel variant, which was added in September 1977, only just scraped into the adequate category. The 3.0-litre

The ergonomically designed dash area of the C123 was shrouded in rubberized plastics and foam with switches recessed – all for safety.

with the carburettor engine was removed from the programme.

Furthermore, on demand, both models were now available with the new hydraulic self-levelling suspension system, ABS (August 1980) and airbag (January 1982).

A comprehensive model improvement package in September 1982, which benefited all 123 series models, hardly left any outside traces on the Coupé. The rectangular wide-band headlamps, the most conspicuous characteristic of the improved variants, had been part and parcel of the standard two-door car equipment from the very beginning. Power steering became standard across the range. From the outside, the improved Coupé could only be recognized by the black (and no more chrome) ventilation louvre in front of the windscreen and maybe by the paint coat, if one of the new eight colour tones was used. Several details were changed on the interior equipment.

In August 1985, serial production of the 123 series Coupés came to an end. In its eight years of production, 99,884 units had been built, 15,509 of which had a diesel engine. The rar-

est version of the series was the 280 C. Fans of two-door exclusive types had to wait for the successor, the Coupé of the 124 series, for more than one and a half years.

Production figures of the 123 series:

230 C	1977–80	18,675
230 CE	1980–5	29,858
280 C	1977–80	3,704
280 CE	1977–85	32,138
300 CD	1977–81	7,502
300 CD TD	1981–5	8,007

W124 SERIES

The Saloon Variant, 1985

The official presentation to the press of the new Mercedes-Benz 200-300 series (W124) took place in Seville on 26 November 1984 by representatives of Daimler-Benz AG

This new **E-Class** followed Sacco's rule of 'homogenous design affinity' with all other models; there were many common features with both the **S-Class 126** and the compact class **W201**.

The trapezoidal rear bootlid shape was at first criticized by the press, but went on to become a design classic.

at the time: Dr Rudolf Hörning, member of the management board responsible for research and development, Friedrich van Winsen, director of the development office, Dr Bernd Gottschalk, director of public relations, and Günther Molter, head of the press office.

During this presentation, a large number of exhibits were used to detail the seven years of work necessary to reach the pinnacle of technique and design that was the 200-300 series.

'This range has given reason and progress a new dimension: a fascinating and convincing ideal, bringing automotive wisdom to the highest level of Mercedes advanced technology.' So said the editor-in-chief, Hellmuth Hirschel.

Official presentation took place at the IAA (Frankfurt International Motor Show) in September 1985. Replacing the successful 123 was always going to be a tall order; however, the 124 was off to a good start as it drew capacity crowds only seen in 1979 with the introduction of the second S-Class 126.

The new range still presented many independent design elements used for the first time and had a functional background true to another Sacco principle – that 'form should follow function'. The characteristic shape of the tail tapering to the end, for instance, and the considerably rounded appearance at the lateral top edges was based on experiments in the wind tunnel, considerably improving the car aerodynamically.

Two further typical design characteristics were the trapezoidal, deeply pulled down bootlid and the inclined inner edges of the almost square rear lights, allowing an especially low loading sill to facilitate the loading of the voluminous boot.

A remarkable, innovative construction detail was the lift-controlled panorama wipers, which gave an 86 per cent wiped windscreen view that was, at that time, the largest wipe pattern in the world. Thanks to a rotational movement overlapping the vertical movement, the upper edges of the windscreen could be wiped much more efficiently than with

The M104 4-cylinder engine on the 124.

The M103 6-cylinder engine was also used in the S-Class 126 series.

the conventional one arm wiper. Electrically heated windscreen washer jets were also part of the standard equipment of all models of this series.

The front and rear axle constructions, already known from the compact class W201, contributed to an excellent driving performance. The new medium-size models were also equipped with a damper strut front axle with individual

The 124 range was increased with the addition of the S124 estate and the C124 Coupé saloon.

A-arm suspension and anti-dive device as well as a multilink rear suspension, in which each rear wheel was led by five independent control arms.

The engines were mostly new developments. Only the 4-cylinder M102 engine came from types 200 and 230 E of the previous W123 series. Besides the completely newly constructed 6-cylinder injection engines with 2.6-litre and 3.0-litre displacement, there was a new diesel engine generation. The 2.0-litre 4-cylinder engine had already been used in the 190 D and the range was now completed by a 2.5-litre 5-cylinder as well as a 3.0-litre 6-cylinder variant.

In 1987, the 124 series model range was again extended. First, two Coupés were presented at the Geneva Motor Show in May, completing the model line-up as a third body variant. Following that, two new saloons were shown at the Frankfurt Motor Show in September: the 300 D Turbodiesel and 300 D Turbodiesel 4MATIC, both using the 3-litre 143bhp 6-cylinder engine that had been introduced in the estates two years earlier. The 4MATIC version was a world innovation; the conventional-drive 300 D Turbo had been part of the sales programme of the American distributorship MBNA since April 1986.

The Coupé Variant, 1987–96

At the Geneva Motor Show in March 1987, a coupé variant of series 124 was introduced, exactly ten years after the presentation of the preceding model at the same place. As with the 123 series Coupés, there was a close technical and stylistic affinity to the saloons. Although based upon the platform of the four-door model, at a glance, however, the C 124 series reveals itself as a vehicle in its own right as a sporty, elegant, individual interpretation of the 124 model series.

The floor plan had been shortened, reducing the wheelbase by 85mm (3in), which underscored the compact, sporty lines of the new coupé. Sides, roof and rear were also redesigned, so that only the front end of the saloon was carried over basically unchanged.

Even though the design required significant and detailed modifications to the body of the four-door vehicle, the Coupé made absolutely no compromises in terms of either active or passive safety standards. To compensate for the absence of the B-pillars, the A-pillars were reinforced internally and also clad in the same high-tensile steel, as were the side sills and doors. For the first time in a coupé, the engineers designed the roof so that the interior of the rearmost section slightly underlapped the rear windscreen, improving both safety and comfort to the rear passengers. Crumple zones that deform according to a specific pattern enabled the C124 to attain excellent ratings for stability and stiffness despite the lack of B-pillars.

A characteristic design element underscoring the independence of the Coupé design from the saloon and estate variants of the series were the rub strips; the saloon version in this early series were simple narrow bands, while the Coupé versions returned to the 'Sacco board' style of the 126 S-Class. These integral side skirts filled the lower part of the body between the wheel cutouts, at bumper

An early design rendering of the 124 Coupé.

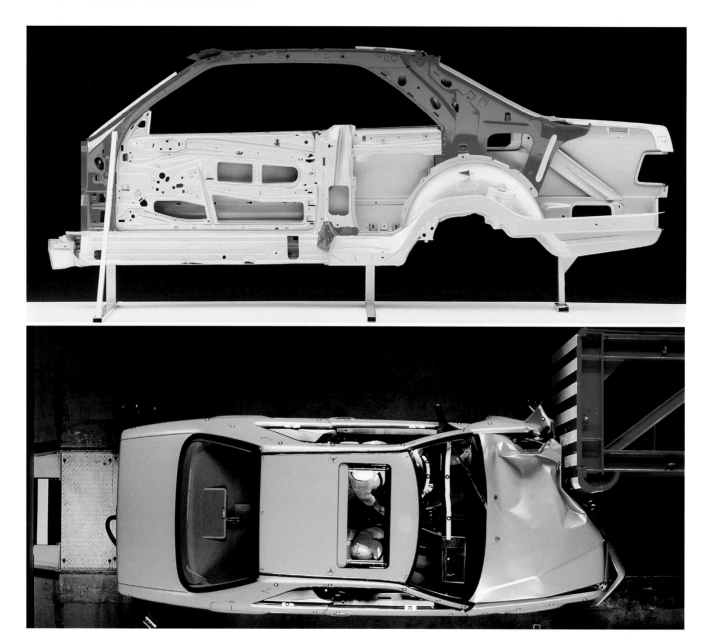

**The built-in safety reinforcement of the C124 gave it better torsional stability
and passenger zone protection than any model previously.**

level, creating an optical link between front apron and rear apron and, similarly to the 126, were painted in contrasting metallic colours.

Where the engineering was concerned, Mercedes-Benz consistently applied a modular principle, so that the Coupé adopted unchanged from the saloon the independent multi-link rear suspension and the shock absorber strut independ-ent front suspension. The braking system also originated unchanged from the saloons.

The range initially comprised models 230 CE (97kW/132bhp) and 300 CE (132kW/180bhp), whose engines were those of the corresponding saloon model. Both units fea-tured a regulated exhaust gas after-treatment system with three-way catalytic converter.

Design Changes

Together with all the other variants of the 124 series, as from September 1988, the Coupé range was equipped with extended standard equipment, now including a heated, electrically adjustable nearside exterior mirror and a windscreen washer system with heated washer fluid reservoir, nozzles and hoses. The ABS (anti-lock brake system), with which all the 124 series were equipped as standard, was already standard equipment in the 300 CE from the outset and in the 230 CE from February 1988 onwards.

In September 1989, Mercedes-Benz presented a fully revised upper medium-class model programme at the Frankfurt International Motor Show (IAA). The refinements focused on changes to the styling of the bodywork and redesign of the interior; thus, on the outside, the Coupés were

The Sacco boards were initially only introduced on the C124 but were later used through most of the model range, including the W140 S-Class.

The facelift of 1989 made improvements in exterior design, such as a chrome strip along the Sacco board top edge and chrome door handle trim.

practically unchanged since they had been equipped from the start with the side rub strips that were the most conspicuous feature of the facelifted 124 model series, and in a way represented the model for the revamping of the other body variants.

The Sacco boards were now optically upgraded with fine polished stainless-steel trim strips that continued along the top of the front and rear aprons. These were complemented by chrome-plated trim elements on the door handles and modified wheel hubcaps. The interior featured upgraded front and rear seats as well as numerous improvements to details.

Together with the facelift, Mercedes-Benz presented a new coupé variant: the 300 CE-24, powered by the 162kW (220bhp) 3.0-litre 4-valve engine of the 300 SL-24 sports cars. The 300 CE-24 became the new flagship model of the intermediate class coupés. Its equipment included light-alloy wheels, power windows, leather-clad steering wheel and shift lever knob, burr walnut wood trim and courtesy lights in the doors.

From June 1990, the Coupé was produced with the tried-and-tested 2.0-litre 4-cylinder engine: the 200 CE (90kW/122bhp), although this engine was exclusively reserved for export to Italy and, later on, to Greece and Portugal.

Into the 1990s: Engine and Exterior Changes

In September 1992, Mercedes-Benz once again revised the intermediate class model range; by this time, two million vehicles of the 124 series had already rolled off the assembly line.

If the emphasis had been on styling changes in the first facelift in autumn 1989, this time Mercedes-Benz concentrated on the engine and appointments.

The engine range of the Coupé models was completely converted to 4-valve technology. Two 4-cylinder units with 2.0- and 2.2-litre displacement from the newly developed M111 series replaced the 2-valve-per-cylinder units. These new engines were distinguished by increased output and higher torque over the entire engine speed range; at the same time, they had lower fuel consumption. The smaller engine developed 100kW, the larger 110kW. An increase in the volume of the catalytic converter reduced pollutant emissions.

With the introduction of the new engines, the model designations changed: the 230 CE became the 220 CE, while the 200 CE export model, which also got the 4-valve-per-cylinder engine, was able to retain its name because the displacement was virtually identical.

The 6-cylinder models, the 300 CE and 300 CE-24, were

The final facelift of 1992 saw mostly engine changes, but a few exterior appointments brought the model in line with the upcoming W140 S-Class.

**From 1993, all 124 models received the inset radiator grille, along with the
Mercedes star on the bonnet (instead of up front on the grille).**

removed from the sales range and replaced by the 320 CE.
Its 3.2-litre 4-valve engine, which had been providing good
service in the S-Class for the previous one-and-a-half years,
was developed from the existing 3.0-litre 4-valve unit of
the M104 series and bore the same series number, but had
changed dimensions for bore and stroke.

All 4- and 6-cylinders now had the same bore, an advan-
tage for more flexible, economical production. The rated
output of 162kW was the same as that of the old 4-valve
unit, but it was reached at 5,500rpm and thus 900rpm earlier; the peak torque was much higher and was also shifted
towards the lower engine speed range.

Apart from the new engine range, the model refinements
included distinctly upgraded standard appointments for all
models of the intermediate class.

A driver airbag and electrically adjustable exterior mirrors on both sides were part of the standard specifications
from October 1992 on. Central locking and a five-speed

transmission, which were included in the basic equipment
of the saloon and estate at this time, had been standard
equipment items in the Coupé from the very start of their
production.

In June 1993, all series 124 models were stylistically
updated, bringing them into line with other model series.
The most striking feature of the modified vehicles was the
radiator grille. This so-called 'integrated radiator' had a
much narrower chrome surround compared with the previous design and was harmoniously integrated into the bonnet; and, just as on the new S-Class W140 range, the Mercedes star sat on the bonnet.

The changes to the light units could not escape notice: the
front direction indicators were given colourless glass covers
and the tail lights bichromatic covers that were coloured a
uniform white-grey in the area of the indicators and revers-
ing light. The yellow indicator light at the front and the rear
was produced by orange light bulbs.

With the merging of AMG and Daimler, a new flagship C124 was offered, the E36 AMG.

Changes also were made to the wheels and the bumpers. The steel disc wheels got new hubcaps in a six-hole design, and the protective mouldings on the bumpers now were painted the colour of the other detachable parts. In addition, the protective strip on the rear bumper was extended to the wheel cutouts.

As the redesigned models went on sale, in June 1993 a new nomenclature came into effect for the 124 series. In line with the S-Class and the new 202-series C-Class, the intermediate class now was called the E-Class. The model designations, too, now followed a modified system in which letters documented that a car belonged to a certain class. The letter(s) were followed by a three-digit number that was still based on engine displacement. The 'E' formerly used as suffix indicating an injection engine was dropped since carburettor engines now belonged to the past.

Mercedes also dispensed with categorizing body variants like coupé and estate with a 'C' and 'T' since they were obvious anyway.

Under the new nomenclature, the two-doors now were called the E220 Coupé and E320 Coupé; the model plate, however, only documented the class to which the model belonged and the engine displacement.

From September 1993, a new, sportier coupé was introduced in the E36 AMG. The engine was created at AMG using the M104 production engine with 3.2-litre displacement. Its bore was enlarged to 91mm, the stroke to 92.4mm. Alongside a four-speed automatic transmission with a final drive ratio lowered to 1:2.82, it produced 200kW from its 3.6-litre 4-valve engine.

With discreetly enlarged chassis fairings, the new flagship Coupé of the 124 series also contrasted stylistically with its less dynamic sister models. Front spoiler, side skirts and rear apron were painted the colour of the car and harmoniously integrated into the body shape; rounding it all off were standard-fit light-alloy wheels (17in diameter) in AMG design.

To offer less performance-minded customers a more

reasonably priced entry-level model, the general sales range was extended in December 1994 by the E 200 Coupé, which delivered 100kW and had previously (since mid-1990) been built exclusively for export to Italy, Greece and Portugal.

Production of the 124-series E-Class Coupés came to an end in March 1996, nine years after their debut at the Geneva Motor Show. In all, 141,498 units were produced in Sindelfingen, around 40 per cent more than previous models of the C123 series.

For coupé lovers, the end of production was sad news, since the market launch of the successor models was not planned until summer 1997.

Production figures for the 124 series:

230 CE	1986–92	33,675
300 CE	1986–92	43,486
300 CE-24	1988–92	24,463
200 CE	1990–2	7,502
300 CD TD	1986–95	5,921
200 CE/E 200 (M111 engine)	1992–6	7,848
220 CE/E 220	1992–6	12,337
320 CE/E 320	1992–6	13,768
E 36 AMG	1993–6	Unknown

CLK GTR C297, 1998

In 1993, while Peugeot achieved a second success in a row with its 905S, the 24 Hours of Le Mans saw the return of the GTs. The 1993/94 season was a failure due to mechanical problems, but the following years marked a glorious period, a golden age of the GT spirit. For a start, 1995 was an incredible year, with the introduction of the McLaren F1 GTR derived from the road version that won the day.

In 1996 and 1997, manufacturers were much more interested in the GT1 regulations, contributing to a successful 1998 and 1999.

GT1 models are in reality prototypes in disguise. Some have a family resemblance to everyday cars, and this is the case with the Mercedes CLK-LM, which managed to humiliate Porsche and McLaren for two years.

The reason it fits into this book about coupés is that to satisfy the FIA regulations, it was also necessary to be able to build at least twenty-five copies of a road version; so in 1997, a prototype of a road version was presented, showing the good intentions of Mercedes and allowing the engagement of the racing versions that year. In April 1997, 128 days after its conception, the first CLK GTR made its first laps

FIA GT Championship in Laguna Seca, California, 26 October 1997. Bernd Schneider won with his Mercedes CLK GTR racing touring car.

at Jarama in Spain: the Mercedes-Benz CLK GTR was born. It retained the saloon-style front grille and dashboard taken from the CLK and was to be manufactured at Mercedes' sports subsidiary, AMG.

Design

Contrary to appearances and its name, the Mercedes CLK GTR was in no way derived from the Mercedes CLK coupés (W208). The very sleek 'racing' design of the Mercedes CLK GTR was the work of Gerhardt Hunga and his team.

Compared to the competition model, some elements were adapted for more harmony as a road-going vehicle. The rear spoiler, for example, was notably more elegantly integrated, while the smaller wheels forced the designers to redesign the wheel arches. The interior offered more comfort and cosseting, and the doors opened like those of the Mercedes 300 SL or Mercedes 300 SLR of the 1950s. An air duct was placed on the roof to provide cool air to the engine intake. The mirrors were positioned farther forward on top of the front wing above the wheel arches.

The body itself was fitted with several air intakes to supply various mechanical components with fresh air. The rear apron featured an air extractor to increase ground effect and grip.

Entering the cabin required a little gymnastics because you had to cross the large sill extrusions, but, once in place, the driver would immediately notice that the dashboard was very much inspired by the Mercedes CLK series apart from being covered in Alcantara-type material. There was no gear lever in the centre console as gear changes were effected via paddles located behind the steering wheel. Overall, the finish of the interior was far from spectacular, in fact hardly even comparable to that of the CLK production models, and it was often criticized as being too 'classic' in style for a supercar of this rank and, of course, price. Fortunately for the passengers, air conditioning was fitted automatically because the cramped cabin very quickly became stiflingly hot. The absence of a boot compartment was slightly mitigated by adding two small storage compartments under each hinged door and a set of fitted suitcases was provided with the car. A radio was also provided.

The CLK GTR's carbon-fibre monocoque is stably connected with a steel roll-cage. The car only weighs 1,000kg (2,200lb), can speed up to 345km/h (214 mph) and is also supplied with MOT approval.

TOP: **Swing-up gullwing-style doors aided ingress and egress although it was still far from easy to step over the deep sills sections.** BOTTOM: **The rear cover could be completely removed for easy mechanical access.**

Engine

Mercedes spared no expense with its engine, starting with the latest 6-litre M120 48-valve V12 that powered the R129 SL 600. This time around, the engineers of Affalterbach (AMG) had nothing to do with the design of the engine, which rather came from English engine manufacturer Ilmor, who were already involved in the production of Mercedes Formula 1 engines. The goal for Ilmor was not just speed but torque. First, the displacement was increased from 5987 to 6898cc. The engine block was lightened by 30kg (66lb) with the use of sophisticated materials: titanium connecting rods, forged pistons, lightweight flywheel. The cylinder head was also seriously revised from the original with larger valves and redesigned camshafts. The 394bhp of the original V12 of the SL 600 roadster was now 612bhp at 6,800rpm and, just as importantly, made 775Nm (572lb ft) of torque at 5,250rpm. This engine, now designated the M297, achieved a maximum speed of 320km/h (200mph) with a 0–100km/h time of 3.2 seconds, and could achieve 200km/h (124mph) in less than 10 seconds.

Mercedes AMG had finally abandoned its tradition of successful automatic gearboxes for a 6-speed sequential gearbox. Paddles behind the steering wheel allow you to click gears in a matter of seconds

As a homage to the W198 300 SL, the bucket seats were covered with a tartan-style upholstery.

Chassis Frame

As we have seen, there was no technical kinship between the production Mercedes CLK (W208) and the Mercedes CLK GTR. Weight and stiffness are still the two main lines

The GT 112 racing engine of the Mercedes CLK GTR (FIA GT series), 1997. The 441kW (600bhp) 6.0-litre V12 mid-engine racer was designed in close co-operation with the racing section, AMG.

Because of the use of light yet strong materials, the weight of the Mercedes CLK GTR remained a mere 1,545kg (3,406lb), allowing agility, excellent road-holding and performance.

of work for engineers on sports cars – even more so on racing cars – and the chassis frame was all race-car sport designed. It consisted of a very rigid and strong carbon-fibre shell weighing only 87kg (192lb). The shell incorporated front and side crumple-zoned areas to absorb energy in the event of an impact. A tubular cage grafted onto a cross-member above the engine compartment was also provided.

The suspension system, too, was all competition car, with superimposed wishbones and coil springs, and a 'traction control system'. The size of the rims and tyres compared to its competition sisters were reduced but remained appreciable, with 295/50 ZR18 at the front and 345/35 ZR18 at the rear. An anti-lock braking system with four 400mm ventilated and perforated discs enabled the brakes to provide lightning slowdowns at high speeds.

In 1998, each of the twenty CLK GTRs costs a huge €1,700,000, and even to date this hasn't changed to any great extent. It cannot, however, be serviced at your local Mercedes-Benz main dealership. There are special AMG technicians made available who travel directly from Affalterbach to maintain and repair your CLK GTR.

Originally, it was planned to build and sell twenty-five coupé versions but, after having difficulty selling just twenty copies, it was decided to 'boost' the market and offer a roadster version (actually a Targa). It had the desired effect and Mercedes

Due to lacklustre sales of the **CLK GTR** coupé versions, it was decided to revamp the car as a 'Targa roadster'. This one belonged to the Sultan of Brunei.

immediately sold six additional units. A little later, HWA offered existing owners the possibility of 'upgrading their Coupé to a 'Super-Coupé' by fitting the 664bhp M297 7.3-litre engine that had been built for the Pagani Zonda.

208 SERIES CLK COUPÉ, 1997–2002

Mercedes-Benz had provoked quite some excitement in March 1993 with a coupé study that avowedly was to set new standards in close-to-series design. For the first time, a completely new interpretation of the Mercedes' bold 'face' was shown, which was characterized by two pairs of elliptical headlights, more strongly moulded wings and a slender radiator grille. The characteristic 'four-eyes' theme influenced the design of the 210 series E-Class and the CLK Coupé on a large scale, especially after the extremely positive reactions of the visiting public at the Geneva Motor Show.

The style and design of the CLK were largely derived from the Coupé study shown in 1993, but the public had to wait until 1997 for the concept car to become reality in the CLK Coupé (C208). The production model bore an uncannily strong resemblance to the Geneva concept.

In 1998, the CLK Coupé was followed by the convertible version and the CLK now became a small product family in

its own right. The technical platform and some components were supplied by the C-Class.

The CLK Coupé was primarily developed at Daimler-Benz as an entirely independent model family, a fact that is expressed in the series designation CLK 208. From a technical standpoint, the CLK was based in many regards upon the W202 C-Class saloons, using their complete floor assembly and other components to keep costs down. The individuality of the CLK, however, was clearly visible in numerous deviations from the detail accomplishment and finally in the fundamentally different body design. Immediately recognizable was that the headlights followed the E-Class W210 with their double round style. Adverts at the time asked the customer to 'Look at Mercedes through NEW EYES'.

Even with it using the W202 platform, the CLK had a much more sporty, younger-looking and elegant design. It even abandoned the hard-top body without the centre pillar of its predecessor.

The Mercedes-Benz CLK had its world premiere, this time in North America at the International Auto Show in Detroit in January 1997. The European premiere took place one month later at the Amsterdam International Motor Show AutoRAI, and shortly thereafter the new coupé series was displayed at the Geneva Motor Show, to mimic its 'concept sister' in 1993.

This new model coupé hit the market in June 1997, at the

Early renderings of the C208 designs.

Close to the final shape, the C208 was built in 1:5 and 1:10 scale clay models.

**Looking at Mercedes
through 'new eyes'.**

The C208 retained the sleek look of its siblings but gained the B-post.

For the first time, practicality was considered in the coupé model, with split seating arrangements and access from the boot.

same time as the C-Class saloons and the estates, both rich in models, and was offered in a new line of design and equipment options, just as the models of the C- and E-Class. The offer comprised the 'Sport' and 'Elegance' versions, with some differences in external details. The Elegance model line had chrome trims surrounding the side windows and slender chrome mouldings at the door handles as well as light-alloy wheels in five-spoke design. The Sport variant reinforced the dynamic impression of the CLK Coupés by putting aside with these ornamental elements and being equipped with forged light-alloy wheels in seven-spoke design.

The CLK was surprising rich in standard equipment even with the new design: all models were equipped with acceleration skid control (ASR), an exterior temperature indicator, a leather-covered steering wheel, remote boot release and heat-absorbing glazing. The new 'Easy Entry System', which moved the front seats automatically forward, considerably facilitated boarding and exiting for the rear passengers. The two rear seats were individual for extra comfort, while the backrests folded in proportion of one-third to two-thirds to allow for easy through-loading from the spacious boot, which then became even more capacious.

Safety Innovation

The new CLK models were also equipped with a number of advanced technological innovations, however, improving safety features, comfort and economy. Above all, there was the driving authorization system ELCODE to protect against theft, which was operated by an electronic door and ignition key. The electronic 'Brake Assist' (BAS) enhanced the ABS by significantly reducing stopping distances in an emergency. The system sensed emergency braking and immediately automatically applied the maximum braking power in a matter of milliseconds. Both systems, ELCODE and BAS, were constituents of a high-performance data network that enabled a rapid and reliable communication between the control elements in the engine compartment and the passenger cabin.

Another novelty, the 'Active Service System' (ASSYST), improved the economy of the car by constantly analysing the oil quality in the engine. The on-board computer assessed how the car was being used and then established when the next service or oil change was needed, thus meeting the engine's exact needs and keeping trips to the service bay to an average of every 18,500–20,000km (11,500–12,500 miles) instead of constantly every 15,000km (9,000 miles).

As was the norm now for Daimler Mercedes, 'passive safety' was at the forefront; the CLK already fulfilled all the requirements in force in crash tests from 1998 within the European Union as well as the future US regulations. When developing the new model line, a great deal of work was put into safety for both the pilot and passenger. The CLK not only had frontal airbags for the front seats as standard equipment, but also side-bags in the doors, and seatbelt tensioners with tension limiters for the front seats. However, for the first time in any production vehicle, the frontal structure of the CLK was designed so that in the event of a crash, its structure was able to dissipate the crash energy for the other vehicle involved as well – a detail that offered maximum protection

Full head-on crash tests were undertaken, not to just match US regulations but to top them.

The C208 off-centre impact test helped to produce a vehicle with unbeatable safety.

to all occupants, but especially beneficial for occupants of smaller or less safety-compliant vehicles.

New Engines

In Germany, the CLK was first available with three different engines: as the CLK 200, with a 136bhp 2-litre 4-cylinder unit already used in the C-Class and the E-Class; as the CLK 230 Kompressor, with the 193bhp 2.3-litre supercharged 4-cylinder engine, also known from the C-Class; and as the CLK 320, with a totally new 224bhp V6 engine that was introduced in the E-Class at the same time.

In January 1998, the 208 series gained a new addition when the CLK 430 with V8 engine was presented at the North American International Auto Show in Detroit. In the same month the 205kW (279bhp) top-of-the-range model had its European premiere at the International Motor Show in Brussels, and was introduced onto the market in June at the same time as the CLK convertible, which had its world premiere in March 1998 in Geneva.

The CLK Coupé, like the SLK and the SL, was built at the Bremen plant but, despite the use of all available production capacity, extremely strong early sales unfortunately led to waiting periods. Even more troublesome was that delivered vehicles were changing hands very quickly at exceedingly higher than retail prices.

Between 1997 and 1999, 110,000 Coupés left the factory, doubling the sales of the C124. The so-called conquest rate of the attractive model series was also astonishingly high. Mercedes-Benz manage to 'poach' around 40 per cent of customers of other car brands.

THE C208 SERIES 2

By August 1999, Mercedes-Benz had significantly upgraded the design, technology and equipment of the entire CLK model series. Both the Coupé and Convertible received the same technical innovations that had provided greater driving safety and ride comfort in the E-Class of the 2000 model year. Altogether, the designers and engineers upgraded around 800 components of the C208 and, unusually, more than 200 of these modifications were visible.

The CLK 430 V8 became the range topper a year prior to the facelift, proving the C208 was here to stay.

The expanded standard equipment included newly designed bumper aprons in the front and rear, side skirts and protective strips in the vehicle colour, exterior mirror housings with integrated indicator repeaters, vertical and horizontal electric adjustment of the front seats, seatbelts in front with automatic comfort-fit feature, a central display in the instrument cluster, a multifunction steering wheel for operating the audio units and telephone, exit lamps in the doors, the 'Audio 10' RDS car radio, the ESP Electronic Stability Program, cruise control and SPEEDTRONIC. This upgrade of the standard equipment continued Mercedes-Benz's persistent value-for-money strategy with the CLK as well. The cost to the customer came to about DM 2,500.

As previously, two individual design and equipment lines were available for the facelifted CLK. Mercedes-Benz replaced the previ-ous 'Sport' line with the more exclusive 'Avantgarde', distinguished by 16in light-alloy rims with a seven-spoke design, door handles in vehicle colour, blue-tinted glass, bird's-eye

The subtle upgrades to the C208 included lower sill mouldings and a different, lower nose vent on the front bumper. The rear bumper received slight flares to the lower section, wrapping around the sides, and different-shaped exhaust exits.

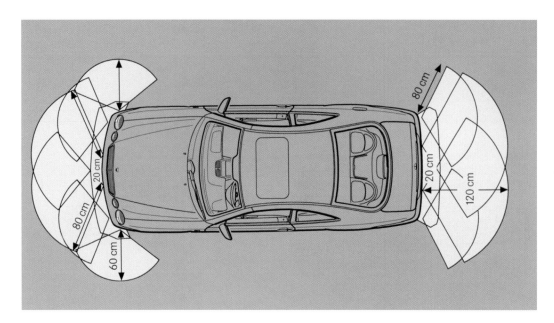

Bumper sensors aided parking through the COMAND system.

The ESP (Electronic Stability Program) detected the onset of unstable driving conditions and countered them by specific wheel intervention through the braking system.

The COMAND system used GPS through a screen display in the dash.

maplewood trim and grey-coloured dials in the instrument cluster, among other features. For the interior, three colour combinations were available for this model variant.

The CLK models of the 'Elegance' line differed from the 'Avantgarde' model by their 16in rims with a five-hole design, door handles and window frames with chrome plating, burr walnut trim and anthracite-coloured dials in the instrument cluster. Four colours were available for the interior appointments.

The five-speed automatic transmission, standard on the V6 and V8 models, was equipped with the practical Touch

shift feature, which in 'D' facilitated manual selection of the five gears.

The list of optional extras also contained innovative new developments from the E-Class and S-Class, especially the new COMAND operating and display system, which combined car radio, navigation system and CD player. Instructions from the electronic traffic pilot appeared in the form of a map on a colour display in the centre console and as icons on the central display in the instrument cluster.

The CLK 55 AMG

At the top of the CLK model line from August 1999 was the CLK 55 AMG, whose suspension and drive technology corresponded to the then safety car of the Formula 1 World Championship. The core of this high-performance coupé was a V8 engine developed by Mercedes-AMG, with 255kW (347bhp) of power and a respectable torque of 510Nm (376lb ft), available at engine speeds between 3,000 and 4,300rpm. The CLK 55 AMG accelerated from 0 to 100km/h in 5.4 seconds and covered the standing kilometre in just 24.3 seconds. The fuel consumption was 11.7ltr/100km (24.2mpg; NEDC overall consumption).

The AMG engine was based on the 8-cylinder engine of the S 500 and had extremely good torque characteristics. Compared with the Mercedes Benz CLK 430, the CLK 55 AMG was lower by about 25mm and fitted with firmer shock absorbers, reinforced stabilizer bars and modified springs. Four large vented disc brakes with diameters of up to 334mm guaranteed optimal deceleration. The ESP (Electronic Stability Program) was also part of the standard equipment of the high-performance Coupé.

AMG light-alloy wheels and 17in tyres boosted the sporty appearance and contributed to the good road-holding of the Coupé. Mercedes-AMG had upgraded the body design with a front apron with integrated front fog lamps, dynamically shaped side sills and a special rear apron. Seats, door panels, sport steering wheel and automatic transmission selector lever were covered with fine leather, with two-tone leather available as an optional extra. Multi-contour backrests for the driver's and front passenger's seats, seat heating, automatic climate control and stereo car radio were other standard-fit details in the interior of the Coupé, enhancing both safety and comfort.

Further Upgrades for the 4-Cylinder Models

In June 2000, the 4-cylinder models of the CLK received the modified M111 EVO engines and as standard received the

The CLK 55 AMG.

The M113 V8 engine developed by Mercedes-AMG produced 347bhp.

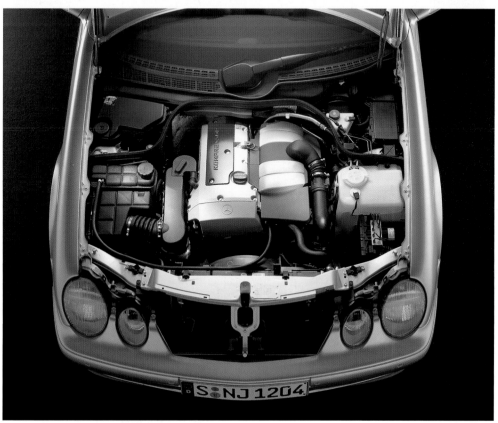

The uprated **EVO** 2-litre Kompressor engine now generated 163bhp. Although down on power, there was no loss to performance figures and fuel consumption was reduced by 15 per cent.

The M111 EVO 2.3-litre Kompressor engine in the C208/2 generated 197bhp.

six-speed manual transmissions. The V6/V8 models, CLK 320 and CLK 430, remained unchanged.

The CLK 200 Kompressor introduced a new 2.0-litre engine with mechanical supercharger, already familiar from the SLK and the new C-Class. This new engine generated 120kW (163bhp) and accelerated from 0 to 100km/h in 9.1 seconds; top speed was electronically limited to 223km/h (139mph).

Even better driving performance was afforded by the CLK 230 Kompressor with its modified 2.3-litre engine that generated 145kW (197bhp); 0–100km/h was recorded as 7.9 seconds and maximum speed was 235km/h (146mph).

With a low fuel consumption of 9.6ltr/100km (29.5mpg; NEDC overall consumption) the CLK 230 Kompressor thus achieved a performance level comparable to the high level of a 6-cylinder engine.

The two 4-cylinder engines were further developed with an eye to future emissions and noise limits and had over 150 of their components improved. They included the cylinder heads, distinguished by flow-optimized intake and exhaust ports with oval cross-sections for better cylinder charging. The same purpose was served by a new, more compact combustion chamber design, which additionally reduced heat loss and thereby improved the response characteristics of the catalytic converter.

The camshafts of the 4-cylinder engines were fitted with special Hall sensors, which determined the position of the piston in the first cylinder for better actuation of the corresponding injection valves during a cold start. The result was significantly improved starting characteristics of the cold engine. Also new was the electric radiator fan that supplied the engine with cooling air and could be controlled in the interest of low fuel consumption and low noise emissions. The air flow components and the intake manifold were modified for acoustic comfort, while a cover over the intake manifold further lowered noise emissions.

The mechanical supercharger was also a new development, contributing audible progress. Thanks to a novel type of bearing technology, uncoupling of the compressor during idling was no longer necessary, so the electromagnetic clutch between the engine and charger also became superfluous. Absorption dampers in front of and behind the compressor also helped reduce noise.

The 4-cylinder models of the CLK were standard-equipped from June 2000 with the new six-speed manual transmission, distinguished by short-shift travel and low shift forces. The state-of-the-art five-speed automatic transmission continued to be optionally available, with the practical Touch shift as a standard feature. In transmission position 'D' it facilitated manually engaging gears one to five: the driver needed only to move the selector lever slightly to the left or right for the transmission to change to the next speed. A five-speed automatic transmission with Touch shift was standard on the CLK 320 and CLK 430. Cruise control with variable speed limiter was standard with all engine variants.

In spring 2003, the CLK Coupés of the first generation were succeeded by the entirely newly developed 209 model series. By May 2002, the Bremen plant had manufactured a total of 233,367 units of this successful model. That was 65 per cent more than the Coupés of the 124 model series, which had been in production for nine years and not just five like the series 208 Coupés.

Production figures for the 208 Coupés:

CLK 200	1996–2002	45,890
CLK 200 Kompressor	1997–2002	15,985
CLK 230	1996–2000	37,479
CLK 320	1997–2002	68,778
CLK 430	1998–2002	22,660
CLK 55 AMG	1999–2002	3,381
CLK 200 Kompressor EVO	2000–02	24,639
CLK 230 Kompressor EVO	2000–02	14,550

CHAPTER NINE

A NEW DAWN: THE FOUR-DOOR SALOON COUPÉ

Even though the CLS C219 went into production with the SL-style grille, so can officially be included in the sport coupé category, it deserves a special mention here as it became the crossover model from the saloon to sport coupé genre. This also heralded the beginning of the disappearance of the famous 'saloon-style grille' on all but the S-Class range of cars.

The Mercedes-Benz CLS-Class four-door coupé was brought to market at the start of October 2004. It was based on an innovative vehicle concept that, for the first time, combined the elegance and athleticism of a coupé with the comfort and functionality of a saloon. It had all the space, luggage volume and everyday practicality you would expect from a saloon, along with the exciting lines that reflect the emotional character of a coupé. With this unique combination, the CLS-Class was one coupé generation ahead.

Essentially, its appeal was largely due to the impressive proportions of its body: dynamically shaped overhangs at the front and rear created an elegant extension to the body, contrasting with the flat, arching roof of a thoroughbred coupé. Designer Hans-Dieter Futschik said, 'The hallmark of modern Mercedes design is the interplay between tautly drawn lines and soft, naturally rounded surfaces.'

The CLS-Class embodied this design approach perfectly: the high belt line of the coupé, which exudes a sense of security, was underscored by a prominent shoulder line that took its cue from the dynamic, rounded form of the front wheel arch, stretching along the entire length of the body before merging effortlessly into the elegant rear light cluster and flowing gently down to the bumper. This distinctive feature allowed the designers to achieve the perfect balance between lines and surfaces. At the same time, it also helped to create an impressively elongated appearance, thus further enhancing the sporty elegance

Although no longer a coupé in the traditional sense, the CLS used the typical design cues of the high rear swage lines and just added two extra doors.

The elongated style of the **C219 CLS** kept that sporty 'grand tourer' feel,
and early design renderings show the saloon-style grille.

The new **CLS** was based upon the platform of the **W 211 E-Class.**

**Daimler based the C219 CLS on the 2010 concept shooting brake. If a coupé
could be a four-door, it could also be a utility vehicle.**

of the body. As a result, from the side, the large, unruffled surfaces of the doors and rear wing formed a contrast to the frameless side windows and low stance still typical of a two-door coupé.

When asked to describe the distinctive look of the four-door coupé, Peter Pfeiffer said: 'In the CLS design there's no such thing as a straight line,' and later, according to *Auto Bild* magazine, added: 'This is no normal Mercedes-Benz; it's a real designer piece. This coupé looks stunning even when it's standing still, with the high waistline and narrow-look side windows emphasizing its sporting credentials.'

Marketed by Mercedes as a four-door coupé, the CLS was designed by Michael Fink in 2001, who also styled the first-generation CLK, the C-Sport Coupé and the Maybach 57 and 62. In Germany and throughout Europe, the model name followed the coupé nomenclature and kept C219, while in the USA the CLS was more commonly named as the W219 model.

Based upon the W211 E-Class platform, the C219 CLS shared major components, including the engines and transmission, and has an identical wheelbase of 2,854mm (112in).

Debuting at the 2004 New York International Auto Show, the CLS quickly established itself as a modern automotive icon and created an entirely new market segment.

After the success enjoyed by Mercedes-Benz, other car makers launched four-door coupés in its wake. In autumn 2009, the second generation of the CLS (C 219 series) made its debut at the Paris Motor Show, further underlining that the coupé concept had now changed irrevocably in the minds of the customer. If a coupé could now be a four-door saloon, it could also be a 4×4 or SUV. The result of this was that, like birds flying south for winter, drivers around the world started flocking to crossover vehicles in unprecedented numbers, which in turn has meant auto makers are introducing more crossover utility vehicles (CUVs) to meet market demand.

At first glance, the shooting brake could be a fast SL Coupé.

Once again Daimler were at the forefront of the movement, and at Auto China in Beijing in 2010, a completely new concept was introduced: the concept coupé shooting brake. Taken from a British automobile type, the shooting brake, it was an exclusive crossover vehicle that combined the luxury and style of a coupé with the luggage space of an estate.

The proportions were clearly those of a coupé: the long bonnet, narrow-look windows with frameless side windows, the dynamic roof sloping back towards the rear – all created a basic stance from which it looked ready to sprint. Only when taking a second look did it become clear that the shooting brake concept car had four doors and an estate rear. The design study revealed its philosophical kinship with the four-door CLS Coupé, which, as already stated, established a new market segment in 2004 and by 2010 had already taken up an incredibly special place in automotive history as a design icon. In retrospect, equally ground-breaking importance might one day be attributed to the concept shoot-

ing brake too, which adopted ideas of the Fascination concept car, presented in 2008, and projected these into the future.

Professor Gorden Wagener, chief designer at Mercedes-Benz at the time of the presentation of the concept car in April 2010, said: 'The shooting brake concept car is based on the great tradition of a stylish, cultivated sportiness which has always characterized the great Mercedes Coupés, and it takes this unique legacy an exciting step further. At the same time it points the way towards the future design idiom of Mercedes-Benz.'

The side profile of the shooting brake concept car was dominated by the low, frameless side windows. Thanks to the positioning of the outside mirrors on the belt line, the side line was emphasized, and all-round visibility improved in the region of the A-pillars. The side windows were supported on a high belt line, which sloped towards the rear in a fresh interpretation of the classic 'dropping line' of iconic

The shooting brake C218 was made available alongside saloon models in all-wheel drive and AMG variants.

Mercedes coupés. An additional exciting touch was made with the prominent, muscular hip points, which forcefully supported the side line. This interaction gave the impression of a sprinter, poised in the starting blocks, ready to release an explosive forward surge of energy. The roof followed through to the rear and dropped away in typical coupé fashion.

The shooting brake models went on sale from October 2012 – as class C218, not under the C219 code – and were available alongside saloon models in all-wheel drive and AMG variants.

The success of these vehicles has undoubtedly come at the expense of other segments. The coupé class has really diminished over the years, though not solely because of the ongoing crossover craze. Motorists can still get a car with two doors, but they are a tough sell. The market has voted with their wallets and most buyers in search of a mid-sized car want them with four doors. The coupé was always seen as the sportier alternative to the saloon; however, things are no longer so black and white. Even mainstream family cars have better performance than most coupés from twenty years ago, providing a great driving experience without sacrificing versatility.

There is no crystal ball as to where it will go from here, but the Mercedes-Benz coupés are, and always will be, a lifestyle statement on wheels.

MILESTONES OF MERCEDES-BENZ DESIGN

1886 Karl Benz presents the world's first car in the form of his patented 'motor vehicle for operation by gas engine'. The structure of the three-wheeler, which is inspired by the design of a bicycle, is an expression of engineering in its purest form.

1900 The Mercedes 35 HP establishes an independent form for the automobile and is regarded as the first modern car. The honeycomb radiator that is organically integrated into the front of the vehicle becomes a hallmark of the brand.

1906 The Daimler-Motoren-Gesellschaft in Untertürkheim sets up its own body manufacturing shop.

1909 The famous 'Blitzen-Benz' (Lightning Benz) record-breaker and racing car is the first vehicle whose design is clearly influenced by aerodynamic considerations.

1910 A defining point is reached in the development of auto-motive design: a bulge below the windscreen, referred to as a 'cowl' or 'torpedo', links the chassis and engine box assembly with the body and passenger compartment to form an organic whole. With its new, smooth walls and continuous belt line, the automobile now has a harmonious form.

1911 In parallel with the flat honeycomb radiator, DMG develops a second characteristic radiator form – the pointed radiator that is used principally for the sporty and high-power models in the range.

1920 The DMG factory in Sindelfingen starts manufacturing Mercedes bodies.

1932 Hermann Ahrens takes charge of the special vehicles department at the Mercedes-Benz Sindelfingen plant.

1934 With the elegant, flowing lines of its Hermann Ahrens-designed body, the type 500K and its 1936 successor, the 540K, represent a highlight of Mercedes-Benz design, especially in the Special Roadster version, which is regarded as the ultimate dream car of the 1930s. The coupé variant establishes the modern coupé tradition at Mercedes-Benz.

1953 The type 180 with its integral body structure is the model that brings the classic Mercedes-Benz design into the modern era. The wings and headlamps are fully integrated into the main body, which also encloses the engine compartment and the luggage compartment at the rear. Above this rises the passenger compartment, which has a large window area by the standards of the day.

1954 This year sees the advent of the legendary 300 SL with gullwing doors, new, unconventional proportions and a new, flat form of the Mercedes-Benz radiator grille, which becomes a defining feature of the front design of the SL sports cars. This super sports car is the last word in auto-motive design in its day.

1957 The vertical headlamps with integral indicators introduced in the 300 SL Roadster become a defining stylistic device in the front design of Mercedes-Benz passenger cars until the beginning of the 1970s.

1959 The Mercedes-Benz 220, 220 S and 220 SE 6-cylinder saloons make their debut with restrained tailfins that are officially described as 'guide bars'. The 'Tailfin' Mercedes is also the world's first vehicle with a rigid occupant compartment and energy-absorbing crumple zones – attributes that mark the beginning of a new chapter in the field of safety technology.

1961 The two-door coupé variant of the 220 SE has its own distinctive design treatment, a notable characteristic being the absence of the saloon model's tailfins. The clean lines of the timelessly beautiful coupé dominate Mercedes-Benz design in the 1960s.

1963 The 230 SL appears with surprising new proportions and lines – as well as the unmistakable 'pagoda roof', a removable hard-top whose special form not only looks good but also offers greater rigidity and therefore safety.

With its clear, geometric lines, the Mercedes-Benz 600 sets new standards for the class of exclusive and luxurious prestige vehicles.

1971 The new 350 SL sports car model and the S-Class of 1972 give visible and tangible expression to the integrated safety concept and define the look of Mercedes-Benz passenger cars. Important design elements are the generously sized, horizontal headlamps, the indicators that can be seen clearly both from the front and the side, the ribbed tail lights and the reach-through door handles.

1975 Bruno Sacco succeeds Friedrich Geiger as head of the styling department and thus becomes the new head of design at Mercedes-Benz.

1979 The design of the new S-Class combines traditional elements with new forms that have been developed as part of the aerodynamic optimization process: defining features include the rising belt line, the integral bumpers and the tapering rear section.

1982 Mercedes-Benz presents the compact class in the form of the 190 and 190 E models. The design of the new compact model series, which is the forerunner of today's C-Class, represents the consistent continuation of the principles that shaped the S-Class. The rear rises noticeably above the lower belt line of the body – a design choice that is initially regarded as somewhat controversial by the public, but is subsequently recognized as a timeless defining feature.

1984 The new W124 medium-size model series has a boot-lid with an almost V-shaped rear face that makes for a low loading sill while maintaining a high-level aerodynamic spoiler lip. The V-shape is framed by the tail lights and is later picked up by other model series and successor generations as a characteristic styling element.

1991 With the new S-Class, Mercedes-Benz presents a new interpretation of the radiator grille – the defining element of the brand. The new model has an integrated radiator that is incorporated in the bonnet.

1993 As part of the first major product initiative, the Mercedes-Benz coupé study causes a stir at the Geneva Motor Show. This is the first showing of a completely new interpretation of the Mercedes face, with four elliptical headlamps.

For the first time, Mercedes-Benz presents the C-Class, the successor to the compact class, in four different design and equipment lines in which the interior design plays an especially important role in expressing the particular character of the chosen variant.

1995 The new E-Class is the first series production model with the ground-breaking twin headlamp face. The new type of front-end design is also adopted in other model series.

The design range offers Mercedes-Benz customers with particularly discerning taste countless possibilities for combining exceptional paint finishes, extra-soft leather in exclusive colours and trim elements with surface finishes in fine wood, piano lacquer, stone and leather.

1996–7 The Mercedes-Benz product initiative sees the advent of numerous new model series, such as the SLK, the CLK, the A-Class and the M-Class. Mercedes-Benz design develops innovative design solutions for these fundamentally new vehicle concepts.

1998 The elongated, coupé-like profile of the new S-Class symbolizes the new forward-looking brand image of Mercedes-Benz. New standards are also set by the interior design, which harmonizes perfectly with the sportily elegant lines of the body. It exudes a strong sense of character, lightness and luxury. The side indicators, which have been moved into the mirror housings for the first time, become a defining styling feature.

1999 Professor Peter Pfeiffer succeeds Bruno Sacco as head of design.

2003 The Vision CLS attracts an extremely high level of attention around the world when it is unveiled at the Frankfurt Motor Show. The concept of a four-door coupé that offers a high standard of long-distance comfort for four occupants immediately generates an enthusiastic response. The 'Autonis' design prize and the 'Most Attractive Study 2003' title reflect the extent to which this innovative vehicle succeeds in capturing the imagination.

2004 The CLS enters series production in almost unchanged form in the course of the second major Mercedes-Benz product initiative. With its unique personality, and its ability to combine the characteristic elegance of a coupé with a high degree of practicality, it conquers new customer groups. Distinctive design characteristics, such as the side feature line, the new headlamp design and the way the rear drops away, set new precedents. The systematic translation of the outside lines to the interior makes the CLS a perfect example of the harmony between interior and exterior design, which is such a characteristic of the brand.

The second phase of the product initiative also sees the introduction of a new, extended design vocabulary. All model series share clearly identifiable familial traits yet each also has its own, characteristic formal signature at the same time.

2005 The S-Class sets new design trends with its almost purist form. With its clear, precisely defined lines and tranquil surfaces, it embodies the new design style in a striking way.

2007 The C-Class is the first Mercedes-Benz saloon to appear with two distinct faces: the Elegance version has the classic radiator grille with the Mercedes star as the radiator emblem, while the Avantgarde by contrast has a grille with a central star – a contemporary interpretation of the air intake used in the 300 SL of 1954.

2008 Professor Gorden Wagener becomes head of Mercedes-Benz design.

Mercedes-Benz brings a breath of fresh air into the compact premium SUV segment with the GLK. The angular basic lines are a homage to the G-Class, the brand's off-road classic.

2009 The E-Class appears with a new, multiple prize-winning avant-garde form with an arching rear wing treatment as a contemporary interpretation of a design element from the integral body structure Mercedes of the 1950s.

The striking design of the new Mercedes-Benz SLS AMG super sports car immediately evokes a sense of excitement, with its long bonnet, the flat passenger compartment positioned well to the rear and the short tail with its extending rear aerofoil. The gullwing doors also recall the legendary 300 SL sports car, as do the wide radiator grille with the central star and the wing-like transverse fin as well as the gills on the bonnet and the sides of the vehicle.

2010 The F 800 Style, with which the Mercedes-Benz designers have reinterpreted and developed the characteristic design idiom of the brand, provides an impression of the luxury saloon of tomorrow. The long wheelbase, short overhangs and elegant, flowing roof line give it a stylishly sporty look. Inside the F 800 Style, fine wood surfaces and plenty of light create a light, contemporary feel.

THE COUPÉ EXPLAINED

THE MODERN COUPÉ

Through the years, numerous styles of coupé have debuted, including the controversial four-door coupé. As the market shifts, the coupé goes in and out of popularity, depending on what is important to consumers at the time.

PRONUNCIATION OF COUPÉ

In English, there are two common pronunciations. The first is 'koo-PAY', which is the anglicized variant of the French-derived spelling coupé (meaning cut). During the 1950s, Chevrolet attempted to appeal to the higher class with their two-door hard-top and their Sport Coupé, which used the French pronunciation.

The other way Americans pronounce coupé is by saying 'KOOP'. This is the pronunciation without the accent and only containing one syllable. It did not always sound like this and the change occurred over time during World War II.

COUPÉS IN THE MODERN AGE

1977 Mustang II Ghia: the demand for a variety of automobiles increased as the need to accommodate large families became more pressing. This is when the coupé was overtaken by the saloon and other family vehicles, such as vans and wagons. In 1977, the International Standard ISO 3833-1977 said a coupé had a closed body design, limited volume in the rear, a minimum of two seats with at least a row, two side windows and doors, a fixed roof with a portion that could open, and a possible rear opening.

During the twentieth century, several models had four doors but were marketed as a four-door coupé. Automobile enthusiasts were not all convinced that they deserved the coupé title. Even Edmunds guide to car values does not list a four-door coupé when they discuss various car models.

At the beginning of the twenty-first century, coupés saw the worst sales of any other category. This is when previously popular coupés such as the Pontiac Firebird and Dodge Avenger ceased production in America.

Today, the sport coupé has made a comeback. People want more performance than before, and they are willing to dispense with space for the extra precision and handling that a smaller car provides. While the coupés of today look nothing like the early versions, they still hold a special place in the heart of drivers. With more than a hundred years of coupés behind us, it will be interesting to see what the next century holds.

COUPÉ VARIATIONS

Manufacturers use the term coupé to define several varieties.

Berlinetta

This sporty two-door car was lightweight and typically only had two seats, but occasionally offered two-plus-two seating. The original meaning was the 'little saloon'. The term itself was coined in the 1930s but was popularized in the 1950s by Ferrari. Later, other European manufacturers, such as Opel, Maserati and Alfa Romeo, used the label as well.

There was a Chevrolet Camaro referred to as the Berlinetta, which was produced from 1979 to 1986. It was aimed at the luxury market and came equipped with an upgraded interior and soft suspension.

Business Coupé

This two-door automobile either had no rear seat in it or a removable one. It was intended for salespeople who needed to travel or vendors that required room for their gear. These coupés became popular during the late 1930s. A few had rumble seats that folded down from the boot space. By the early 1940s, the size of the business coupés had grown even larger, making even more cargo room. Chrysler had an extensive collection of models during this time with large boots.

After World War II, some business coupés began to have small back seats, perfect for a couple of small children. The last true American business coupé was the AMC Gremlin in the 1970s. It came at a time when people wanted a cheap car and were not worried much about fuel economy.

Club Coupé

The club coupé was a two-door vehicle that featured a larger rear seating area for passengers compared to the two-plus-two automobile. It still had two doors, but the front seats tilted forward to allow passengers into the rear section.

The early club coupés weren't American made, but French. The term came from a design like the exclusive club car in a train, resembling a parlour or lounge-type setting. They were the perfect combination of a sporty coupé and roomy saloon, and also weighed less than a four-door model: the 1952 Kaiser, for example, was 25kg (55lb) lighter than the saloon, representing a 2 per cent drop.

Four-Door Coupé

The four-door vehicle has a roof line like a coupé in the rear. This lower roof design allows for less passenger seating and headroom than a typical saloon. The first vehicle to receive the designation was the Rover P5 in 1962. Production lasted through 1973. Then other cars took the classification as well, including the 1985 Toyota Carina ED, a 1992 Infiniti J30 and the 2005 Mercedes CLS.

Mainly the term was used for marketing purposes. The press liked the idea of having four-door coupés and was happy to label cars as such, including the 2009 Jaguar XJ. Overseas, other vehicles took the classification as well, including the Volkswagen Passat CC, the BMW F06 and one five-door coupé, the Audi A7.

Opera Coupé

This two-door coupé was designed to drive to an opera. They offered easy access to rear seating and featured a folding front seat located next to the driver. There might also have been a special compartment used to store hats. Many of these cars had solid rear-quarter panels with small, circular windows. This allowed passengers to see out without worrying about being seen. This window design was later adopted on many US automobiles throughout the late 1970s into the early 1980s.

Quad Coupé

This is a car that featured either one or two smaller rear doors and lacked a B-pillar.

Hatchback Coupé

A hatchback coupé utilizes a luggage compartment as part of the passenger area. It is accessed through a larger rear tailgate.

Sports Coupé

These coupés have no B-pillar and are often a fastback. They might also be referred to as a hard-top coupé, Berlinetta, Berlinette, or two-door hard-top.

Saloonet (Saloonette)

This fastback club coupé is also called an aero coupé. It might or might not be a hatchback coupé. At one time it was a saloon that looked like a coupé.

Two-Door Saloon

While these cars have as much room and seating as a saloon would, they only have two doors. Even the profile might appear like a saloon. Other terms for these cars include a business saloon, brougham, brougham coupé, club saloon, coach or Victoria.

POSITIONING INSIDE
THE MODEL LINE-UP

Many coupés resemble the auto maker's family saloon but are a two-door variant instead. Other manufacturers create their sporty cars to be completely different from the four-door models. An AMC Matador, from the 1970s, looked nothing like its four-door version, but had distinctive styling and design. Likewise, the Dodge Stratus and the Chrysler Sebring both had saloons and coupés that looked different from each other, and were in fact engineered at entirely separate plants. Some of these cars exist inside a model line on their own. They might be closely related to some of the other models, but still have their own name, such as the case with the Alfa Romeo GT. Some of the vehicles look unlike anything else in the auto maker's line-up, like with the Toyota GT86.

INDEX